THE MOVING FEAST

A cultural history of heritage foods in Southeast Mississippi

by

Allan Nation

**A division of Mississippi Valley Publishing Corp.
Ridgeland, Mississippi**

Grateful acknowledgment is made for permission to reprint the excerpt from *A Gracious Plenty* © by John T. Edge, Center for the Study of Southern Culture.

First printing June 2010
Second printing June 2011
Third printing August 2012

Copyright © 2010 Allan Nation

Library of Congress Cataloging-in-Publication Data
Nation, Allan.
  The moving feast : a cultural history of heritage foods in southeast
  Mississippi / by Allan Nation.
    p. cm.
  Includes bibliographical references and index.
  ISBN: 0-9721597-5-4 (alk. paper)
  1. Food habits--Mississippi--History. 2. Food preferences--Mississippi--
History. 3. Agriculture--Social aspects--Mississippi--History. 4. Missi-
ssippi--Social life and customs. I. Title.
  GT2853.U5N38 2010
  394.1'209762--dc22
                    2010017541

Cover photos by Carolyn and Allan Nation
Spanish West Florida Map by Tony Howe
Cover design by Steve Erickson

Manufactured in the United States.
This book is printed on recycled paper.

Table of Contents

Preface

Southeastern Mississippi makes a particularly good place to study pre-industrial heritage food production because the frontier lasted longer here than in most areas. With no steamboat navigable waterways, until the coming of the first railroad in the late 1880s the interior of this region was an almost totally self-contained local food economy. While the coming of the railroads opened the region to food imports, the use of "fire agriculture" as perfected by the Indians continued here in full force as late as the 1960s as did un-fenced, open-range grazing.

A 19th century French philosopher, Jean Antoine-Brillet-Savorie said, "Tell me what you eat and I'll tell you who you are." This was certainly true in Southeast Mississippi where the local food culture was shaped by the sub-tropical climate, the poor soils and the ethnic backgrounds of the people who lived here. As the early European settlers quickly discovered, the subtropical zone is a unique ecosystem where neither the traditional European temperate crops nor the common tropical crops of the Carribean do well. Consequently, the food culture that developed was a mish-mash of American Indian, African, Carribean and Celtic food cultures.

Few of us have considered the difficulty pre-industrial economies faced in providing a year around supply of food prior to refrigeration and outside food sources. Pre-industrial food cultures reflected what worked in a particular climate and soil type over a long period of time. Therefore, they stand as an excellent guide for food products a modern-day local food culture could and should be built around. When you consider that all of these foods were produced "organically" without any petro-chemical inputs, they are even more impressive.

The reason they didn't need these inputs was because the local agriculture was based upon a planned rotation, or movement, of the crops to avoid weeds, disease and to utilize natural fertility. Hence the title of this book *The Movable Feast*. Crops were moved to "new ground" every two to three years. Cattle, sheep and hogs were "step-grazed" in large herded mobs and were only grazed across an area once every few years. These techniques not only obviated the need for fertilizer but also prevented crop and livestock diseases while producing a year around supply of green forage for the livestock.

These are all techniques that are being re-discovered by the more progressive modern-day "organic" agriculturalists, and were the basis for agriculture in the Argentina pampas until quite recently. Unfortunately, modern-day organic agriculture got branded in the 1970s as something vaguely "left coast" and therefore culturally unsuited for the South. It is my hope that the new "Heritage Food Movement" that is originating in the South and that celebrates this region's food past can be more culturally successful.

This book started as a single article in *The Stockman Grass Farmer Magazine,* which specializes in modern-day grassfed meat and milk production. By the time I had finished the article, it was way too long, and therefore was split over two issues. Those two articles created a lot of feedback from all over the United States for more in-depth information on heritage food production. While this book focuses on the Piney Woods region of Southeast Mississippi, the agricultural techniques described here were similar throughout the southeastern pinelands from southeastern Virginia to eastern Texas and with some small modifications in the hardwood region of Appalachia.

One

The Indians

American Indians have been greatly underappreciated as agriculturalists. Consider that 50 to 60 percent of all plant species grown in the world came from the Indians of North and South America. These include all types of corn known today, cassava, chia, squash, pumpkins, zucchini, pinto beans, lima beans, tomatoes, potatoes of all kinds, avocados, peanuts, cocoa beans, vanilla, strawberries, pineapples, bell peppers, jalapeno peppers, paprika pepper, chili pepper, sunflower seeds, rubber, tobacco, cocoa, manioc and some species of cotton.

What diminished the Indian's claim to many of these was that the Spanish frequently took Indian plants from South America to Europe and later brought them back to North America; thereby, food historians incorrectly claimed them as Spanish derived. For example, the sweet potato was said to have been brought to North America by Columbus from the island of St. Thomas in the Caribbean, however, other historians say the plant was already growing in the American South prior to his arrival. The white potato, which was grown by Indians in the upper South, would not over-winter in the warm winters of Southeast Mississippi, and it was not grown until the 19th century when new slips could be imported by steamboat or rail each spring from farther north.

The first French explorers found the Indians in Southeast Mississippi to be taller than the average European because their diet had much more meat protein in it. Historians estimate

Bathing Beauties

European explorers' stories of the streams in Southeast Mississippi being filled with naked Indian maidens were true.

the male American Indian consumed around 2500 calories of food a day, considerably more than the average European male in the 17th century. They were also much cleaner as the Indians in Southeast Mississippi bathed daily, whereas, Europeans only bathed once or twice a year and shaved equally infrequently.

By the time of European exploration, the Indians in Southeast Mississippi had become quite sophisticated and lived in towns, albeit temporary ones. The earliest French explorers were surprised to find that the Pascagoula Indians lived in European-appearing cabins and slept in raised beds similar to Europeans.

The three major tribes that inhabited Southeast Mississippi were the Choctaws, the Pascagoula and the Biloxi Indians. The word Pascagoula means "bread people" in Indian dialect. The bread referred to was corn bread. The Indians also consumed corn as grits and hominy. Grits and hominy are made by first soaking corn in wood ashes, which loosened the kernel husk. The Indians balanced this high omega-6 fatty acid diet with green wild plants eaten both fresh and as cooked salads. Of these the pokeweed was the most difficult to prepare as its roots and plant stems are poisonous. The Indians would boil the weed's leaves in water several times and then fry it in animal fat with an egg.

Black Bear

The Black bear was the Indians' preferred meat source due its reliably fatty meat, which made it very flavorful. Bear grease produced from boiling bear fat was used to ward off mosquitos, as a hair dressing and to prevent sunburn.

The Indians

Also, the Indians of Southeast Mississippi were pretty sophisticated farmers rather than just hunter-gatherers. In fact, they were far more successful at farming than the French were in Southeast Mississippi. Begging for food from the Indians was the only way the French settlers survived when the British cut off their food imports from the Caribbean during the French and Indian War.

Indian tribes were the originators of the "moving feast" concept of land rotation. Crops were grown in what is termed by hydrologists as the "back swamp" area along the region's many creeks and rivers. The back swamp is an alluvial soil area that annually floods during the winter rains but is normally dry the rest of the year. This annual flooding keeps the soil rich in organic matter and available nitrogen.

Unfortunately, it is an area that in Southeast Mississippi is usually densely covered by large cypress, magnolia and gum trees that put the forest floor into a dark gloom. Therefore, the first thing the Indians had to do to farm these areas was to open the ground up to the sun. They did this by killing the larger trees with girdling. Smaller trees and bushes were cut with stone axes and burned in piles, and their ashes were used as fertilizer. As these stumps suckered new growth, small fires would be built on the stumps to kill the suckers.

Oaks, pecans, chestnuts and hickory trees were spared due to their valuable acorns and nuts, but all other back swamp species in the area to be farmed were purposefully killed with fire and girdling. Apparently, no effort was made to actually chop the trees down as it has been estimated by modern-day anthropologists that it would have taken five men, five days to cut down one sizable gum tree with stone axes. When large

Moving Tribes
The Choctaws had no permanent "capital city." They conducted the business of the tribe wherever the Chief chose to live.

cypress trees were needed for dugout canoes, called pirogues, the tree was girdled, and after it had dried out a fire set at its base and stoked until the tree toppled over. Fire and stone scrapers were then used to hollow out the tree and shape it into a shallow draft boat.

Once the girdled trees dropped their leaves the forest floor was opened to the sun to allow the Indians to plant gardens of squash, melons, corn and beans. Indian corn had a maturity cycle of only two months. This allowed the Indians to grow corn virtually year around in Southeast Mississippi. The English called the small Indian corn "six weeks corn." This short maturity cycle was important because tropical rain events could cause the back swamp to flood and drown a crop. While

Acorns

Acorns were a major food source for Southeast Mississippi Indians. One large oak tree could produce 1000 pounds of acorns per year. The preferred acorn was from the swamp white oak, which was sweeter than the other species. Acorns contain bitter tannins that protect them from insects and bacteria.

The Indians would shuck the acorns of their skins and then pound them into small particles. Boiling water was then poured over these particles and allowed to stand for one hour. This process was repeated until the bitter flavor of the tannins was gone. The acorn particles then had the water eliminated by squeezing them inside a twisted cloth. They were then slowly dried before a low heat fire or in a warm oven after the fire had died. After drying, the particles were pounded into a meal for cooking.

Acorns are high in natural fatty acids and must be used within a week or they will go rancid. Processed acorns taste like a cross between a hazelnut and sunflower seeds. Acorn bread was usually made in small thin cakes and baked on a stone before the fire.

the ears of Indian corn were smaller than modern day corn the kernels were much larger. The ground for each corn plant was hilled to prevent water logging in the swampy soils. These individual hills were as

Sweet Potato Leaves
Indian children used the sugar-filled leaves of the sweet potato plant as a chewing gum.

far as five feet apart to give them access to as much soil nitrogen as their roots could find and to prevent the spread of fungal diseases, which were rampant in the high humidity swamps.

Leguminous climbing beans were planted in each hillock with the corn to provide nitrogen. Planting the corn with a companion legume was found to increase the corn yield three-fold. Wood ashes from the campfires were used to provide calcium, phosphorous and potassium to the plants. No effort was made to control the annual weeds that grew between the corn plants as many of these were harvested for medicinal purposes.

The idea that Indians put a fish in each corn hillock for nitrogen was actually something that the Indians learned from the French and taught the English. This was not a common Indian practice. Their practice was to harvest the soil's naturally built-up reserve of organic nitrogen and then move on after a few years. This necessity of moving was also spurred by the exhaustion of fallen limb wood near the camp. The Indians were very heavy users of firewood as smoky fires kept mosquitos away at night and were used to preserve meat and hides. Early explorers said the smoke of a single ocean side Indian village could be smelled hundreds of miles at sea.

Indian Tobacco
Indian tobacco was much stronger than today's tobacco and it was psychoactive in much the same way that marijuana is. Smoking the Indian peace pipe really made you feel peaceful and was mildly hallucinogenic.

Meat Tenderizer

Indians tenderized meats with paw-paw juice long before it was used commercially.

Because of the virtually year around warm climate, small game such as turkey, rabbits, squirrels, possums and raccoons that could be eaten in a single meal were preferred to the larger game animals. Some historians believe there was another reason the Indians concentrated on small game and that was that these animals were competitors for the acorns and nuts that were an important part of the Indian diet.

Small game were caught in traps or hunted with hollowed out bamboo blowguns and specially weighted throwing sticks that had a rock tied to one end. These sticks were thrown in an end-over-end fashion and were incredibly accurate in skilled hands. As a boy I remember watching teenage Indians hunt rabbits with such throwing sticks. I marveled at how they easily killed a running rabbit fifty feet away.

Meat was normally cooked in an earthen pot over a fire as a stew with corn and beans. Alternatively, it would be skewered on a small green limb similar to shish kabob. One end of this stick would be pushed into the ground adjacent to a campfire. Often this meat would be cooked at very low temperatures for much of the day. Such slow, indirect cooking made even the leanest of game meats very tender. Until the advent of the pig, only bear meat had enough fat to be cooked directly over the fire's coals without becoming tough and dry.

Deer could be a garden pest and were purposely hunted

Weapons

The most coveted European technology by the Indians was not the gun but the steel axe. The Indian's bow and arrow was a far superior military weapon to the smooth-bore, single-shot muzzle-loaders used by the 17th century Europeans. Archery practice began at the age of two.

hard to remove them from near the Indian villages. Pregnant and nursing does were the Indians' primary targets as these two targets reduced deer numbers the fastest. Bison hides were the primary currency for inter-tribal trading. The French would buy both bison and deer hides whereas the English wanted only deer hides. In the warm climate, clothes were primarily made from cool-wearing fiber from the mulberry bush. Winter cloaks were made of bird feathers. The Indians developed a hide tanning process that only required smoke and the brains of the animal. This leather was used primarily for moccasins.

Once the Indians exhausted the soil nitrogen in their riverside gardens, these areas were abandoned and normally volunteered into blackberry and wild strawberry and eventually into dense stands of native bamboo. This bamboo required direct sunlight to grow and was typically found only on what the Europeans called "old fields" or abandoned Indian farms. By the time of European settlement almost all waterways south of the Ohio River were lined with these Indian created bamboo "cane breaks." These canebrakes became the favorite habitat of the black bear and the large "canecutter" rabbit. The bamboo provided the raw material for the Choctaw Indians' beautiful woven baskets and their blowguns.

Hickory Nuts

Hickory nut milk was an Indian favorite. Hickory nuts were pounded to open them, boiled and then strained through many fine strainers so that only a thick milk remained. This milk was said to be as thick and rich as fresh cream and was a key ingredient of Indian hominy and corn cakes. Charles Mann author of the book *1491* described his experience with Georgia hickory nut milk as "ambrosial - fragrantly nutty, delightfully heavy on the tongue, unlike anything I had encountered before." Most Indians are lactose intolerant and cannot digest the milk of animals.

Snakes

The Indians in Southeast Mississippi considered snakes to be sacred animals and refused to kill them even though they were deathly afraid of them. Remedies for snake bites were a core knowledge in Indian medicine.

In addition to their horticultural pursuits, the Indians in Southeast Mississippi were highly proficient "game ranchers." Rather than seeking out game willy-nilly, they preferred to attract, or alternatively drive, the game to them for harvest. They did this through the knowledgeable use of agricultural fire. The tribes of the eastern United States called fire "Our Grandfather Fire" and could not have survived without harnessing it as a major agricultural tool.

Contrary to the movie *Bambi*, large wild animals are not afraid of fire but are attracted to it. The fire releases the minerals trapped in the plants and leaves them readily available to the animals in its ashes. Wild animals greedily lick these ashes, and the smell of wildfire smoke will normally bring them running. Wild animals also know that standing in the fire's smoke will give them relief from biting deer flies and mosquitoes. Consequently, hunting large game always began with starting a smoky fire to attract the game.

The fire's ashes also sweetened the soil and promoted the growth of legumes, which attracted rabbits to the burn and the Indians' pre-set traps. Later the bison would return to graze

Bamboo

Bamboo cane was used for blowguns, arrow shafts, mats, candles, and baskets. To use cane for baskets, a woman would go to a nearby canebrake and collect a number of stems six feet or longer and quarter them. She then peeled off the inside until all the strips were flexible and of even thickness. They were then ready for dyeing and use. Dyes were made from walnuts and many plant roots.

upon the young fresh grass of the burn and could be easily harvested as well. Occasionally setting the canebrakes on fire flushed out the tasty black bear and rejuvenated the stand at the same time. Setting a fire in a circle drove small game toward the center where the Indians waited with snares and blow guns.

The grass around the Indians' village was kept burned short year round to remove chiggers and ticks and to make snakes visible. This precautionary burning not only opened clear fields of fire in case of attack but it also prevented an enemy from setting an offensive fire that could threaten the camp. Burning off an area was a common practice of hunting parties before camping for the evening for similar reasons. Also, setting woodland fires was considered great entertainment. A burning canebrake rivals the best Fourth of July fireworks show for explosions and sparks. Their enthusiasm for fire was only surpassed by their "white brothers" the Scots Irish who took woods burning to an even greater extreme.

The net effect of all of this burning over thousands of years by the Indians was to turn the landscape from a continuous forest into an open, grassy, savannah. Only the fire-resistant oak and pine survived in great numbers on the region's up-

Forests

"It may be said that the general consequence of the Indian occupation of the New World was to replace forested land with grassland or savannah, or where the forest persisted, to open it up and free it from underbrush. Most of the impenetrable woods encountered by explorers were in bogs or swamps from which fire was excluded; naturally drained landscape was nearly everywhere burned. Conversely, almost everywhere the European went, forests followed. The Great American Forest may be more a product of settlement than a victim of it."

Fire in America, A Cultural History of Wildland And Rural Fire, Stephen J. Pyne

Mealtimes

The main Indian meal was served once a day before noon. Men ate first and the women and children ate what was left.

lands. The fire resistant swamps were said to resemble California redwood forests where huge cypress and gum trees soared some 120 feet into the air. Many early explorers used the term "Cathedral-like" to describe the effect of these mature trees. Some revisionist historians are now saying that the upland eastern forest *followed* European civilization rather than preceded it because most Europeans stopped the Indians' fire regime. However, this was not the case in Southeast Mississippi where the Scots-Irish settlers readily adopted the Indian way of farming and ranching and thereby preserved the open grassy upland landscape until the mid-20th century. Historians estimate that this man-created new grassland attracted the Western bison to cross the Mississippi River around 1000 AD. They were found in great numbers all across the Southeast by the 16th century.

The bison is the only ruminant animal that can do well year around solely on the native warm-season grasses common to the Southeast Mississippi uplands. Unique among ruminants, the bison lowers its metabolism during the winter months. This allows it to survive on the frosted standing dry grass of the upland bluestems. The bison also helped keep the land open and largely free of hardwood trees. Bison enjoy the leaves of broadleaf hardwoods and will push over young hardwood trees

Three Sisters

Corn, beans and squash were referred to as the "Three Sisters" by the Indians. Always planted together they were thought to draw strength from each other, much like women in the tribe. The tall corn plant was the centerpiece providing support for the beans that grew up the stalks. The squash grew along the ground and kept the soil moist.

to get at them. This habit helped keep the upland areas pine dominant whereas under natural succession they would have been hardwood dominant.

> **Giving Thanks**
> Indian lore told that a child would be punished with a stomachache if they did not give thanks for their food.

The first French explorers in the middle of the 17th century saw large herds of bison grazing on the grassy Mississippi prairie that stretched northward from the Gulf. The French explorer, Pierre LeMoyne d'Iberville, thought it would be possible to domesticate the Mississippi bison, sheer its wool, and thereby break the Spanish dominance over the world wool trade. Needless to say this idea didn't last longer than the first attempt to sheer a bison. The bison in Mississippi were hunted into extinction by the early 1800s for its valuable hide.

So what did a year around diet look like for South Mississippi Indians?

In Mary Ann Wells book *Native Land* there is an illustration of the Natchez Indians' annual calendar. The calendar is divided into 13 "moons" with an appropriate animal symbol of what they would have been eating at that time of the year. The Natchez dominated Southwest Mississippi, which has a similar climate to Southeast Mississippi so the food groups would probably have been similar.

The first moon - probably February - is a deer symbol.
The second moon is strawberries.
The third moon is little (immature) corn.
The fourth moon is watermelons.
The fifth moon is peaches.
The sixth moon is mulberries.
The seventh moon is great (mature) corn.
The eighth moon is turkeys.
The ninth moon is bison.
The tenth moon is bear.
The eleventh moon's symbol is a wild duck, however, the Indians called it the moon of the "cold meal."

The twelfth moon is chestnuts.

The thirteenth moon is nuts of all kinds.

The Indians were able to steal some pigs from Hernando De Soto during his 17th century trek across the Southeast, and they rapidly became a favorite Indian food. In reverse of the Scots-Irish practice, they penned their pigs and left their gardens unfenced. The Indians also domesticated the wild turkey that they drove in large cross country drives from as far as 120 miles inland to sell to the French in Mobile. Hogs, smoked and dried fish, dried persimmons, dried peaches, and pecans were also major trade items with the French. However, the most sought after food item by the French was clarified bear oil, flavored with sassafras. This was the cooking oil of choice for the fussy eating Frenchmen. In return for food, the French provided the Indians with guns, bullets, powder, steel axes, and woven wool blankets. The Indians were constantly perplexed by the fact that the French preferred to barter for their food when they could have grown it for themselves for free.

The French ceded Southeast Mississippi to England at the end of the French and Indian War (Seven Years War). The French convinced the Pascagoula and Biloxi Indians that the English would enslave them, and in 1764 they followed the French in their retreat to Louisiana. This left only the Choctaw Indians in Southeast Mississippi. As long-time allies of the French, they were lucky the British rule of the region was short.

Of all the Europeans, the Scots-Irish were the Indians'

Early Herds

If you think methane from America's herd of 40 million cows is destroying nature consider that at the time of Columbus North America had 60 million bison, 30 to 40 million pronghorn deer, 10 million elk, 10 million mule deer, and as many as two million mountain sheep. And, this estimate does not even include the white-tail deer, which today still numbers around 30 million.

favorite. No doubt this was because the Scots-Irish readily took to the Indian ways of fire-based agriculture and adopted their practices almost totally. The one thing they missed was that the Indians did not purposefully burn everything, every year. Most ranges were only burned by the Indians once every five to seven years. Infrequent fire rejuvenates nature but a too frequent fire can kill it.

> ## Treaty of Mount Dexter
> By the Treaty of Mount Dexter in 1805 the choctaws ceded all lands in south Mississippi between the Pearl and Pascagoula Rivers. However, Indians living on those lands were not required to leave.

Some historians say that the American idea of democracy came from the early settlers' study of Indian culture. Men and women were considered equal, but were consigned to specified set roles. While men were to wage war, this could not be done without the women of the tribe first agreeing to it.

The Choctaws were allied with the winning side during the American Revolution and the War of 1812 and so avoided the harsh treatment of the tribes that sided with the British. Considered one of the five "civilized" tribes, the Choctaws adopted European customs and dress. Many intermarried with white settlers. While the Choctaws had long made a weak beer from corn, hard liquor was unknown and proved to be a major social problem for them when introduced by white traders.

Mulberry Bark

The Choctaws used the lining around the inside of the mulberry bark to make cloth. The material is beaten to make it stretch and thin out. Several of these beaten sections can be added to increase the size of the material. Designs are added on the cloth by carving cane and painting the cane with dyes and then placing the designs on the material.

The Moving Feast

In 1830, Choctaw Chief Toblachubabee converted to Methodism and decided that the only way to save the Choctaw people was to move to Oklahoma and thereby escape the deleterious effect of the white man's rum. Today, there are only a handful of distinct Choctaw Indian communities remaining in Southeast Mississippi with most living near Philadelphia, Mississippi, in the east central part of the state.

The primary lesson to learn from the Indian period is that the landscape looked very different than it does today. It was not a jungle-like forest of closely-spaced pine trees and a dense understory of brush species. It looked like a well kept park with green forage growing year around. Charles C. Mann, author of *1491* said that if modern man wanted to return as much of the landscape as possible to its state as it existed in 1491, "they will have to create the world's largest garden."

Two
Hide Tanning

For 150 years the production of animal hides would provide the economic underpinnings of Southeast Mississippi.

Human cultures around the world found a wide variety of ways to preserve an animal's hide and make it into useful leather. Some preservative agents used successfully were organ meats, human urine, dog feces, pigeon droppings, fermented milk, butter, eggs, sweet corn, pine nuts and yucca root. North American Indians developed a leather culture that was fully equal to that of Europe's based on using nothing but the brains of the harvested animal and wood smoke.

I can well remember my own Appalachian grandfather telling me after one of my youthful misadventures that I didn't have enough brains to tan my own hide. I had no idea what that saying meant. Now I do.

The Indians discovered that hides could be placed in *flowing* water with no deterioration of the hide and the hair would loosen after three days and three nights of submersion. The hair, flesh and fat could then easily be scraped off with a dull knife. The hide was then *bated*, or softened, by soaking the hide in a solution of brains and water. The wet hide was then walked on barefoot for two to three hours to further soften it. This uncured product was termed *rawhide* leather.

Rawhide leather was kept soft and supple by the frequent application of boiled bone marrow fat, which also made the leather waterproof. The Indians primarily used this type of uncured leather for moccasins. Since these wore out pretty quickly, curing the leather wasn't considered worth the effort.

Buckskin leather was typically soaked in wood ash rather than fresh water and after bating was cured with salt or wood smoke. Salt curing turns the leather yellow (yellow breeches) and smoke curing turns it a khaki to brown color depending upon how long the hide is smoked. The hide is stretched on a frame prior to smoking to prevent wrinkles that would streak the leather due to uneven smoking.

The Indians preferred corn cobs for hide smoking but the Scots-Irish preferred the fresh smell cedar smoke imparted to the leather. Only smoke-cured buckskin leather is washable.

Commercial tanneries using the Indian method often used pig brains for tanning. Interestingly, pig hides were not generally tanned until the advent of a pigskin shoe called the Hush Puppy in the 1960s. An American football is called a pigskin but it has always been made from cow leather.

Ignoring the Indian method, North America soon adopted the European method of using *tan*, or ground up tree bark, to make a long-lasting durable leather. All tree barks contain *tannin* but oak and hemlock are particularly high in it. Preserving hides by soaking them in water and oak bark is thought to have been initially perfected by the Hebrews.

In nature, tannin protects plants from fire, insects and bacteria. It also provides a natural wormer for animals who eat the plant's leaves in small amounts. The production of tanbark was a major industry in the Appalachians in the late 19th and early 20th century. Many of the larger sawmills in that region had adjacent tanneries to add value to their by-product bark.

"To tan a skin is to saturate it with tannin in such a manner as to promote the slow combination of this principle with the gelatine, albumen, and fibrine contained in the former," the 1881 *Household Cyclopedia of General Information* explained. This is done primarily by soaking hides covered with ground bark in water. This process is called *vegetable tanning* and it takes upwards of a month to complete.

Hide Tanning

Today, most tanning is done with chemicals and is called *mineral tanning*. The chemical process produces a preserved, blue-hued hide much faster but also produces a much weaker end product than traditional vegetable tanning. Still time is money and it is estimated that 80 to 90 percent of all the leather in the world is now chemically tanned. The only leather products that are routinely vegetable tanned today are shoe sole leather and leather that will be carved such as Western saddles, scabbards, holsters and western-style belts.

Most American hides are now shipped to China for tanning and then to Vietnam where they are made into shoes for re-export to North America and Europe. Some of the leather is returned here for upholstery and artisan products. Just about the only remaining vegetable tanneries in America are small tanneries used primarily for high value taxidermy specimens.

Unblemished hides are called full grain. Hides that have been patched and pasted to hide defects are called top grain. Every hide reveals the life of the animal. Scratches, horn cuts, tick bites and barbwire scrapes are all very visible. Brands can greatly lower the value of the hide. Currently, only eight percent of all hides can qualify for upholstery leather and only a third of those for the very highest grade of finish.

While leather is priced on a per square foot basis, finished leather is typically sold as full hides. The average size finished steer will have about 45 to 47 square feet of finished hide. In recessionary 2009, full-grain, vegetable or brain tanned hides were offered on the Internet for between $400 and $600. This is roughly double the price of the highest grade chemically tanned hides.

Three
The Europeans

Probably few Americans realize that it was the fashion demand for animal hides that spurred the initial westward movement in American history. This movement was created by a seemingly insatiable European demand for deerskin breeches.

In the 18th century, yellow deerskin trousers were similar to blue jeans in the early 20th century. They were extremely durable and long-lasting and consequently became the symbol of the artisan male. Upper class males seeking a symbol of virility soon began to demand short deerskin breeches that ended just below the knee as was the upper class fashion at the time. Deerskin breeches indicated that perhaps you were a hunter with privileged access to the King's forest and its deer and were therefore possibly one of society's elite.

In the 1700s, all of the deer in England were claimed by the King and the killing of one of his deer without his permission guaranteed you a "year and a day" in prison. Consequently, the local supply of deerskin was extremely limited. Of course when fashion demand meets restricted supply, the price of the base commodity goes through the roof, and so it was with deer hides. With the home market unavailable, the primary source for deer hides became England's North American colonies. In America, deer were plentiful and easily harvested by hunting at night with torches as the deer would freeze in the torchlight. Between 1755 and 1773, Savannah, Georgia, alone exported 2,601,152 pounds of deerskins to England.

During the American Revolution, deerskin breeches combined with a blue wool coat and a homespun shirt became the standard American military uniform. The use of indigenous clothing sources was purposely dictated by General George Washington to

> ## Land
> During the French period land in Southeast Mississippi was so cheap a parcel large enough to support a family cost about the same as a sack of flour.

symbolize America's independence from England. Some elite American forces such as General Dan Morgan's sharpshooters dressed completely in khaki-colored deerskin outfits with deerskin jackets as well as full-length deerskin pants.

Following the Revolution, similar deerskin shirts and jackets became the fashion rage in America. This new domestic demand on top of the continuing demand from Europe caused deer numbers to quickly diminish on the East Coast. Consequently, the hide hunters began their westward trek following the retreating herds of deer.

In the late 18th and early 19th century, deer hides were the most reliable source of income for America's earliest pioneers and actually became a form of currency. The Scots-Irish called an American dollar a buckskin or "buck." But, I am getting ahead of myself. Let's back up 100 years.

The French first settled in what would become Ocean Springs, Mississippi, in 1699 because the Mississippi River was at full-flood and they could find no dry ground to build a

French Land Grants
The French government was so bankrupt in the 1700s that it couldn't pay its soldiers except in land grants. Unfortunately, no records of these grants were kept and this became a major problem in subsequent years for the French settlers. The British recognized French grants only if the grantee actually lived on the property.

Land Purchase

The European families of wayward sons could purchase a "good position" in the colonies for them.

fort on the Mississippi. They knew that control of the mouth of the Mississippi was critical to their goal of fully exploiting the lucrative hide trade in the interior of Canada. However, the French had no serious interest in colonizing the region or in creating an overseas empire. With a large land area and population greatly reduced by the Black Death, the French faced a great push to resettle overseas. What France wanted was to exploit whatever easy wealth they could find to finance their continuing wars with the English and Spanish.

The French totally failed in Mississippi as pioneer agriculturalists. They knew how to farm in temperate France and they knew how to farm in the Carribean but the climatic vagaries of the subtropic region totally baffled them. While the winters were normally warm, occasionally arctic cold fronts would sweep through and totally destroy their tropical crops. In the summer their spring planted wheat would shrivel up and die in the hot summer sun. After each climatic setback, the French only survived by throwing themselves on the kindness of their Indian allies, the Choctaws, until supply ships could arrive

Cast Iron Cooking

One of the most lasting imports of the French period was the large cast iron pot. A heavy iron pot evenly disperses and retains heat without burning the food. This was perfect for the long simmered meals of the Indians and was a popular trade item. The iron also absorbs flavors from one meal and releases them into the next. Consequently, washing a cast iron pot with soap and water was considered a major no-no. The traditional wedding gift in Southeast Mississippi was a large cast iron skillet. Again, the cast iron was merely wiped clean and never washed.

from the West Indies.

At that time, European royalty's income came primarily from duties on imports and exports through ports. This made control of the port of New Orleans at the mouth of the Mississippi a major prize for all the European powers.

The French dependence upon supply ships from France and the French Carribean colonies made them sitting ducks for their arch-enemy, Britain's favorite weapon, the naval blockade. During the French and Indian War in the mid-18th century the French were defeated by the British. In 1763 the French divided their holdings east of the Mississippi River between England and France's ally, Spain. The British got all lands east of the Mississippi and the Spanish all of France's holding west of the Mississippi, including New Orleans. This set the pattern for Europeans conveniently ignoring the fact that the city of New Orleans is actually located on the *east* side of the river, which should have put it in British West Florida, not Spanish Louisiana. Ceding Louisiana to the Spanish was an absolute gift with no payment or conditions attached.

As the peace treaty was written, British holdings were supposed to stop at the 31st parallel, which bisects present-day Lumberton, Mississippi, but the British arbitrarily moved the border north to what would become Vicksburg, Mississippi, and then drew a straight line east to the Chatahoochee River which forms the border of Georgia. A primary aim of the

British Land Grants

British land grants south of the 31st parallel were of three kinds. One granted 100 acres to each head of a household and 50 acres to each dependent. Another was a purchase grant that allowed the purchase of 1000 acres very inexpensively; and the last were 5000-acre military grants given to every retired officer who served in the French and Indian War. Non-commissioned officers were awarded 300 acres and privates 100 acres.

British was to be able to cut Spanish New Orleans off from its food and fuel supplies in the hinterlands via a chain of inland forts and an active naval blockade in the Mississippi Sound off the coast of Mississippi. At that time, large ocean-going ships off-loaded their New Orleans-bound cargoes onto smaller shallow-draft ships at Ship Island, directly south of present-day Gulfport, Mississippi. These small boats then sailed through the Rigolets Pass into Lake Pontchartrain. This backdoor route to New Orleans was much shorter and far easier than sailing up the Mississippi River against its strong current.

Unfortunately for the mostly French speaking, but now nominally British settlers in Southeast Mississippi, New Orleans was their primary market, so they turned to smuggling. The British blockade was very sparse and easy to avoid and actually had little effect on commerce until the onset of the American Revolution.

In 1772, the British gave major land grants in Mississippi to English loyalists in Georgia and South Carolina. Many of these "Tories" moved to the area to escape the wrath of the American rebels during the Revolutionary War. While owning land in Southeast Mississippi, they actually preferred the more genteel environment of Natchez and did little to develop their holdings in the region.

In 1779, during the Revolutionary War, Spain, seeing

The Colonies

At the time of the American Revolution, there were fifteen British colonies, not thirteen. Residents of the colonies of East and West Florida were well pleased with British rule and did not participate in the Revolution. During the war large numbers of Scottish-descent people moved into Southeast Mississippi from North Carolina. Primarily Protestant, they settled in the northern part of Southeast Mississippi, leaving the coastal area predominantly Catholic.

that Britain had its hands full with the American army and the French navy, declared war on Britain and defeated the British in battles at Natchez, Baton Rouge and Mobile. In 1783, British West Florida became Spanish West Florida. To keep the peace, Spain agreed to honor all English land grants in the area if the grant holders would convert to Catholicism. This was later modified to not openly practicing the Protestant religion. Also, in return for a pledge of loyalty to the king, Spain offered even more land grants, promised no taxes for the residents and allowed French and English to continue as the region's primary languages. This very light handed rule was to prevent the Anglos from seeking American rule. Needless to say, the lack of taxes made Spanish rule very popular, and Southeast Mississippi became a major supplier of food and fuel (beef, charcoal and lumber) to the nearby booming entrepot of New Orleans.

The Spanish envisioned West Florida as a giant cattle ranch that could be used to feed their slaves in the Caribbean sugar islands, and brought in Spanish cattle, sheep and horses that adapted well to the region's climate and became the dominant breeds until the1930s. The Spanish also brought sugar cane, and the settlers were taught how to make Moorish style table syrup and an evaporated cane juice brown sugar or *raspudura*. The Caribbean and its long dry cycle in the winter was ideal for the conversion of seawater to salt in evaporation

Pine Tar

The Spanish government offered attractive prices for pine tar to use in caulking ships. Hurricane-downed pine trees rotted away to the fat, pitch-laden hearts of the trees. This wood was gathered and placed in round stacks, and a clay kiln was built over them. The heartwood was set on fire at a small opening. These kilns were always built on a hillside so that the tar flowed downhill into waiting containers. A byproduct of tar manufacture was charcoal, which was in great demand as a cooking fuel in New Orleans.

ponds. This salt was brought to the Gulf Coast and used to preserve beef and hides. The Spanish had found that eating salty beef helped cane field workers maintain their strength in the Caribbean heat.

In 1803, Napoleon asked for New Orleans and Louisiana back from the Spanish. The Spanish agreed but were shocked when Napoleon immediately turned around 20 days later and sold all of the Louisiana territory to the United States. This was highly unpopular in culturally-European New Orleans where the local residents considered up-country Americans rural hicks and country bumpkins.

In turn, the United States was shocked when Spain refused to give up its lands east of the Mississippi and openly began to prepare for war over the issue. With a huge new land mass to digest and massive debts left from the revolution, the United States filed an international grievance against Spain but tried to patch things up with its former ally. Eventually, Spain negotiated its claim down from the southern half of Mississippi and Alabama to only the land east of the Mississippi in Louisiana, Mississippi and Alabama below the 31st parallel, and relations between the two countries returned to amicability.

If you look at a map of the area, you will see the 31st parallel forming the bottom of the states of Mississippi and Alabama with the exception of the two panhandles that reach down to the Gulf of Mexico.

Cotton

Little cotton was grown in Spanish West Florida until the invention of Eli Whitney's gin in 1795. Cotton grown along the Pearl River was floated down the river on flatboats to a place called "The Gin" where it was ginned then loaded onto schooners for New Orleans. On the Gulf Coast a fine, long-staple cotton called "Sea Island Cotton" was grown. This cotton required an extremely long growing season and high humidity but needed little soil nitrogen.

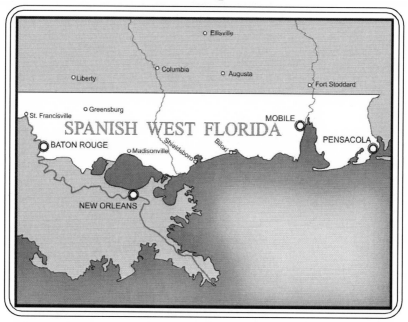

  Those two panhandles plus the part of Louisiana east of the Mississippi and south of the 31st parallel were the final Spanish claim. Again, note that New Orleans lies on the *east* side of the Mississippi River and this was the basis for the United States' claim to the whole area.

  In the end, West Florida was a tiny Spanish colonial toehold on the underside of the United States made up of French, Spanish and Loyalist British Tories, all of whom were, at least publicly, Catholic and whose land claims and wealth were dependent upon the continuation of Spanish rule.

Four
The Africans

The most significant French food contribution to the region was their bringing in African slaves in the early 18th century. Originally from Senegal and Gambia in west Africa, these slaves brought barbecue, eggplants, peanuts, sesame, hot peppers and okra with them. The West African name for okra is ngombo. This proves that you cannot have a true gumbo without okra.

Couscous, an African dish made of cracked grain and meat was the mainstay of the slave's diet in the 18th century. The French encouraged the slaves to plant personal gardens and to raise chickens for their own consumption and sale. Consequently, chicken became the staple meat in the blacks' diet. The Africans taught the Europeans that eating "hot" spicy foods helps people keep cool in hot weather. These same spices have anti-microbial properties that help prevent diarrhea and stomach upsets from meat rancidity. This was very important during the hot weather months.

From the Indians in the Carribean, the blacks learned the art of barbecue. This slow cooking method allowed very lean meats to become extremely tender. The flavor of these lean meats was greatly enhanced with various sweet sauces containing honey and/or cane syrup.

It was in the Deep South that the two major fried food cultures of the world—the Scots and the West Africans—met. These two cultures shared recipes, and the result was "Southern" fried chicken. Beef, pork, fish, and vegetables of all kinds were eaten rolled in corn meal and deep fried.

White women were always in short supply during the frontier and colonial periods. Many white men established liaisons with both Indian and African women and fathered many children by them. Those of partial Indian descent were considered to be "white" while those of partial black descent were considered to be "black."

The term "Creole" literally means a child of European, Spanish, or French descent born in the colonies. It originally had nothing to do with race. Following the Civil War, free blacks who had not been slaves before the war began to call themselves "Creoles" as a way of differentiating themselves from the poorly educated former slaves.

During the French colonial period, Governor Bienville in 1724 made it illegal to separate slave families when they belonged to the same master. Husbands could not be separated from wives nor parents from children. This gave slave families in Louisiana (which included Southeast Mississippi at that time) a place and sense of stability that slaves in other parts of the country did not know.

At the time of the Civil War, 63% of the farmers in Southeast Mississippi owned no slaves and of those who did, the most common ownership was a husband and wife pair. In 1860, 56% of the blacks living in New Orleans were free blacks. In 1860, the number of large slave owning plantations in Southeast Mississippi, so common in Hollywood versions of

Slave Housing

A slave cabin complex was known as the "quarters." Some were laid out as squares and others in a linear design. Slave cabins were crude and sparse. Coarse cloth serving as curtains hung from the open windows and doorways. They slept on crude rope beds or on blanket-covered pallets of Spanish moss, corn shucks or straw.

Holy Trinity

Celery, onions and bell peppers are central to Creole cooking and are called the "Holy Trinity."

the South, could be counted on the fingers of one hand. Consequently, the 1860 African American population of the region at 25 percent of the total was less than half that of the state as a whole.

Not all slaves worked in the fields. Plantation work forces were highly specialized with slaves engaged in cooking, carpentry, barrel making, gardening, blacksmithing and caring for horses and livestock.

Antebellum commissaries were warehouses filled with supplies required by the people who lived on the plantation. Salt, rice, tobacco, potatoes, coffee, flour, leather, seeds, quinine and other medicines and fabric material like linsey and cottonade were their most common commodities.

"The kitchen was usually placed near the 'Big House.' It served the entire plantation and had a garden nearby," according to *Rural Life Cooks*. "Most of the cooking was done in a large open fireplace. The kitchen was typically separated from the main house because of the danger of fire, the heat during the summer, unwanted cooking odors, and noise. The overseer rang the plantation bell around 4:00 a.m., at which time the cook, who was usually a slave, and her helpers began their day in the kitchen. The fire boy started the fire by lifting the fire cover or curfew, or ashes may have been used to cover the

Wood Culture

"Many of the men along the Pearl River made a living by cutting and shipping firewood to New Orleans. All homes of that era were heated by wood. All cooking was done with wood. To supply the city with wood required the labor of many men and boats for its transportation."
Louisiana's Loss, Mississippi's Gain, A History of Hancock County, Robert G. Scharff

embers. Most of the cooking was done with reflected heat, although boiling was done directly over the flames. Breakfast was served in the Big House around 9:00 or 10:00 a.m., dinner in the early afternoon and supper around 8:00 p.m. The slaves' noon meal was prepared in the kitchen but their other two meals were prepared at their own cabins."

"Through the years, there always seemed to be a black hand on the Southern skillet," wrote John T. Edge in *A Gracious Plenty*. "Granted, there were exceptions, homes where the meal made it from field to table by dint of sweat from a white brow. But more commonly, in columned homes of pretense and dogtrot cabins alike, black backs bent to heft the kettle from the stove, black arms flexed to beat the biscuit dough on the stump, black fingers plucked the feathers from the chickens... Jim Crow laws may have dictated where blacks could go to school and with whom they could consort, but in the kitchen the black cook was able to express a sort of subversive creativity, slipping in a pepper pod here, an okra pod there. In the kitchen, freedom of expression was tolerated, even encouraged. As a result, the foods of the South were reinterpreted, in an Africanized manner, by African American cooks."

Following the Civil War, the black percentage of the population in southeast Mississippi continued to fall until the lumber boom in the late 19th century.

During the log-rafting era when this was the only way to get the logs to mills, a lot of the logs went floating down the

Healing Herbs
Herbs were gathered while in blossom, left to dry, crushed and kept from the air. Sage was used for headaches. Summer Savory relieved colic. Green Wormwood treated wounds. Hyssop was used to treat colds and lung problems, and flax seed for coughs. Motherwort was believed to calm the nerves and Catnip was taken for fever. Thoroughwort was given for problems of indigestion.

stream until the first turn and got hung up. Others sank. Many were stolen by log rustlers who changed the log owner's brand. Around 1856, the coastal mills began hiring rafters to put the individual logs floating downstream into large rafts and then bringing these down to the mills. Log rafting would continue on the region's rivers until around 1910 and was one of the highest paying cash jobs in the pre-railroad era, one that paid blacks at the same rate as whites.

The premier rafter on the Black Creek was a seven-foot-tall black man named Wesley Fairley. A former slave and Union Army veteran, Fairley had befriended a Confederate prisoner at Ship Island named Lorenzo Nolley Dantzler. After the war, Dantzler inherited a small sawmill in Moss Point, Mississippi, and encouraged Fairley to supply it with logs. By the 1880s the mill had grown to be one of the largest in Mississippi and Fairley was one of its largest suppliers with many black and white employees.

The limbs of the harvested trees would be lopped off and stacked in a cross-hatch pattern and then a mud kiln built around them with only one air access hole and a chimney hole at the top. The limbs at the top of the kiln would then be set on fire and a "collier" would control the amount of air with a wide board to create a smoldering fire that would slowly turn the tree limbs into charcoal. This was a major export item to New Orleans where it was sold as "house fuel."

Pecan Thrashing

In her memoir of Laura Plantation near Vacherie, Louisiana, Laura Locoul Gore recalled that as a child she sometimes joined the sugar plantation's slave children in collecting pecans. An older slave who was experienced at climbing trees, would begin at the top and work his way down, all the while thrashing the branches with a bamboo cane. The pecans were then collected in barrels—twelve or thirteen a time —and shipped to New Orleans for sale.

Another fuel export to New Orleans was "lighter wood." This was the heart of the pine tree after the outer soft wood had rotted away. This heartwood was full of resin, and consequently burned with a very hot flame. Centuries of hurricanes had left the forest floor littered with such hot-burning heartwood and it became the fuel of choice for steam boilers and ovens in the region.

My wife's father's family had a commercial bakery in New Orleans. Her father told me his earliest job was going to the Basin Canal during World War One and buying lighter wood fuel wood from the schooner captains from Mississippi. Lighter wood was also sold in bundles of six-inch-long sticks that were used to start stove wood or coal. Hence the name, lighter wood.

This pine heartwood was also very rot resistant and was used for fence posts, house and bridge supports. It was said to last "three score years" before rotting.

Drawn by the lumber boom, blacks from Georgia and the Carolinas moved to Southeast Mississippi in large numbers to work in the sawmills and fast growing turpentine industries. Unlike sawmill work, which attracted both blacks and whites, turpentine work became almost exclusively the work of blacks,

Clabber

Milk from the cows on Laura Plantation was poured into yellow bowls where it was allowed to clabber, or naturally sour and thicken without a separation of curd from whey. The next morning the cream was skimmed off and used to make butter, which Laura Locoul Gore never enjoyed, preferring the "yellow, rancid butter from the country store." The cream was put in a wooden churn until it turned to butter. She noted that since the slavery era the Negro children were always given the excess milk and clabber, dished out by a dining-room girl from a table at the back of the house.

and in both the black and white communities no group of people had lower status. In many ways, slavery was a kinder system than working in a turpentine camp.

Each camp had a commissary where the workers drew supplies and provisions against the money payments due them for their labor. In many areas, cash payments were only made once a year at the Christmas holidays. Loans were made throughout the year against this pay.

The commissary owners encouraged the workers to buy things they did not need and were not above fraudulently adjusting the books. However, a worker could not leave a camp until his debts were paid. Indebted workers who ran off were forcibly brought back and forced to work off their debts to the commissary through their labor.

The workers lived in villages or "quarters" owned by the company. In these villages, the supervisors meted out justice without the interference of local law enforcement. The death of the workers from fights and arguments was seldom reported to the law. It was the policy of the operators to bury the dead and save the living due to chronic labor shortages. Many workers who accepted the harsh life of a turpentine camp were escaped convicts and outlaws from other regions. People of both races tried to avoid going near the camps out of fear of them. The operators and woods-riders who oversaw the work always carried pistols as protection from their workers. Turpentining was said to be "outlaw work carried on by outlaws."

Blacksmith
The blacksmith could make nearly any metal object the community needed and did much more than just shoe horses. They could mend cartwheels, repair chains, drill clock weights and lightning rods and make most of the tools used in local farming and construction. The blacksmith was also frequently involved in barrel and wagon wheel manufacturing.

The Africans

As during slavery, the workers were encouraged to grow their own vegetables and to hunt and fish for food on Sunday, their only off day. Squirrels, possums, raccoons, skunks, rabbits and turtles were especially relished. The workers were issued a weekly food ration consisting of a peck of unbolted corn meal, four pounds of smoked pork, and a quart of cane syrup. The worker prepared his next day's meals in the evening after work. Supper was the heaviest meal of the day and consisted of meat, syrup and cornbread. Workers arose at four thirty in the morning and would stop for a breakfast of cold cornbread and syrup around eight or nine.

In logging camps, the kitchen force consisted of a head cook and his helpers who were called flunkies or cookies. A competent cook was expected to be able to prepare food for 80 to 100 men. One flunky to 25 men was the general rule. The cost of feeding men in the remote logging camps averaged from 45 to 65 cents a day and was a major expense for sawmill owners.

In the large scale sawmills, mill workers were provided with a breakfast and lunch and worked twelve- to fourteen-hour days. The L. N. Dantzler Lumber Company provided meat with its meals but was the only lumber company in the region that did so. In 1880 the pay for a fourteen hour day was one dollar. In 1895, the majority of those engaged in manufacturing, logging and rafting in the region were African-Americans. In 1899 there were 16,491 sawmill workers in the state. In 1904, there were 24,415 and in 1909, 37,178.

Due to the on-going labor shortages in the region, African Americans were allowed to take jobs in logging that were traditionally considered "white" such as operating steam locomotives and steamboats. Some steamboats on the Pearl River had all black crews.

Five
The Celts

Now, I must regress a bit to bring in the next big impact in the cultural and food history of Southeast Mississippi, and for that we must look at the history of western Pennsylvania.

The first world war did not occur in 1914-1918 but between 1754 and 1763. This war involved both North America and Europe. In Europe, it is called The Seven Years War and in the United States it is called the French and Indian War. In what would later become the United States, the French preferred to let their Indian allies do most of the fighting while they used French troops to defend their hold on Canada.

In Europe at that time, battles took place on battlefields to avoid civilian casualties. Enlisted men weren't allowed to shoot at enemy officers and no one aimed their weapons, firing them from the hip rather than the shoulder. Battles were sort of large chess games with minimal casualties and the losers of wars were always well-compensated with small countries for being good sports.

However, the American Indians had no concept of a war between gentlemen and fought a brutal, no-holds-barred type of guerrilla warfare. Some of the worst of this type of warfare was in western Pennsylvania and the German and English settlers there just didn't have the stomach for this barbaric form of war. However, the British found their Celtic settlers and soldiers did. The Scots, Ulster Irish and Welsh quickly adapted to this type of unstructured warfare and even relished it. As a result, the

English began to flood the Pennsylvania frontier with Celts, including one young Scottish draftee, Edward Nation, my family's first American antecedent.

The Celts could not only fight like Indians, they could live like Indians, and after the war readily adapted to the Indian life of hunting. Adopting the Pennsylvania German settlers' super-accurate long rifle, they headed West following the retreating herds of deer and their treasured hides.

According to the book *Fire in America* by Stephen J. Pyne, the Appalachian region at that time was not a dense forest but more of an open savanna of grass and widely spaced oak trees. This open landscape was the result of the Indians' use of fire to attract and flush game and the trampling and pushing down of young trees by the huge herds of bison that grazed in tight herds for protection from predators.

The Celts were graziers of cattle and sheep and like the Indians saw trees as the enemy of grass. They had used frequent fire to remove the forests of Scotland and Ireland and in America they became even greater firebugs than the Indians. This enthusiasm for fire soon brought them into cultural conflict with the English and German settlers who had no such fire culture in their backgrounds. The English and Germans saw plowing the earth as the only true agriculture and disdained

Settlers' Homes

Frontier preacher Hamilton W. Pierson described the homes of the early settlers in Southeast Mississippi as a log house of less than fifteen feet square, that typically contained a loom, a narrow table, a couple of chairs, two benches and a corner bed. A large fireplace was built at the front end of the room. The midday meal was typically barbecued pig, ashbed-roasted sweet potatoes, graham bread, bee-tree honey and coffee. Following Celtic tradition the men ate first, while the women served and looked on in silence.

Backwoods Preachers

Backwoods preachers preached mightily against false pride, sin of any stripe, general debauchery, and specifically, tobacco chewing, whiskey drinking, and cavorting with girls.
Mississippi's Piney Woods, Thomas D. Clark

open range ranching. The Celts love of graziering, and particularly their use of autumn stockpiled pasture rather than hay as winter feed, was seen by the English and Germans as proof of the inherent laziness of all people of Celtic descent. Consequently, the Celts became very sensitive to overt signs of disrespect, often violently so. Following the American Revolution, the great tide of westward surging humanity split. The English and Germans settled the "good soil" northern states and the Celts, now self-described as "Scots-Irish," turned south practicing Indian-style, fire-based agriculture. My family's Scots-Irish history reflects this diaspora.

Edward Nation had four sons. Following service on the American side during the Revolution, they left Pittsburgh and headed west. Two of the four went to Kentucky, one went to all the way to Missouri and one went south to the mountains of north Georgia. My family tree is the Georgia branch. Now back to Spanish West Florida.

Following the American Revolution the United States

The English and the Celts

The North was settled mainly by Englishmen and was culturally dominated by them, and the South was settled mainly by Celts and was culturally dominated by them. A list of Piney Woods traits most observed by contemporaries reads like an inventory of traditional Scottish, Irish and Welsh cultural characteristics. Celts had been pastoralists since antiquity, and they continued to be pastoralists in the American South.

facilitated the westward movement of settlers into the interior by building "military highways." One of these ran just north of the border of Spanish West Florida near present-day Hattiesburg and the Scots-Irish followed it. They began settling the border area as hide hunters and graziers.

Unfortunately, all of the rivers in this area ran south through Spanish territory and Spain put a 12% tariff on all American goods that crossed the border. This infuriated the tax hating Scots-Irish and they quickly turned to smuggling and plotting another revolution.

At that time, Spain promoted immigration to Spanish West Florida to all Catholics regardless of national origin. The largely Protestant Scots-Irish crossed their fingers when taking their vow of loyalty to the Pope and the King of Spain and moved across the line in significant numbers. Their goal was to build enough numbers of Scots-Irish inside of West Florida to be able to eventually overthrow the Spanish and allow the tax-free movement of their hides, cattle and logs to the Gulf. These trouble makers were called filibusters by the settlers loyal to Spain.

By 1810 the Scots-Irish had enough numbers to make their move. Spain had its hands full with a revolution in Cuba and had less than 100 soldiers in the whole of West Florida. These demoralized soldiers had not been paid in two years and put up little resistance.

Land Prices

In 1803 Congress passed a special preemption act for land south of Tennessee that allowed settlers who had lived on their claims by October 1795 the right to purchase up to 640 acres at the minimum price of two dollars per acre. After 1820 the price was lowered to $1.25 an acre. This price would remain the base price of unimproved land in Southeast Mississippi until the 20th century.

The Moving Feast

The West Floridians then formed an independent republic and petitioned the United States to take them in as a territory. Embarrassed by the whole affair the United States waited 74 days to see if Spain was going to move militarily against the rebels, and when they saw the Spanish weren't willing to fight for West Florida, the United States annexed the area "as provided for by the 1803 Louisiana Purchase."

However, the Spanish did not leave and the United States did not press its claim for another two years. Between the Pearl River and Mobile, there existed a complete government vacuum with no law enforcement. Into this vacuum rushed pirates and thieves of all kinds who preyed on commerce in the Mississippi Sound. Using fast, shallow-draft boats these pirates could retreat into the shallow waters of the Pearl and Pascagoula deltas where their pursuers could not follow.

The still resident Spanish authorities became almost as corrupt as the pirates and made land grants to speculators who did not qualify under Spanish Law. These grants were made until 1812 and resulted in claims being made for most of the alluvial soil regions along the Pearl River. Legal disputes over these and the prior British land grants turned most new settlers against land ownership, and an open range, frontier culture would persist in Southeast Mississippi long after that of the West had ended.

The motto of these newest Americans was "Neme me impune lacessit" in Latin. This loosely translates into "Nobody

Dogtrot

The dogtrot house features two rooms of equal size divided by a central breezeway that was usually half the room's width. Each room had a fireplace at the outer end. The front and rear porches were also half the width of the rooms. The dogtrot was the most common house of the Scots-Irish across the South as it was comfortable in the greatest range of temperatures.

> ## Trade Goods
> "The family raised livestock, made charcoal, crushed seashells for lime, and boiled seawater for salt. These items were all valuable for trading with other settlers and with the Indians."
> *Twelve Flags, Triumphs and Tragedies,* Dale Greenwell

messes with me and gets away with it." Extremely sensitive to disrespect, they were quick to settle matters with their ever-present dirk knife. Lead and powder were too expensive to waste on an argument.

The West Floridians assumed they would become a part of Louisiana or an independent state. However, the United States federal government divided West Florida among the state of Louisiana, and the territories of Mississippi and Alabama. This provoked howls of anguish.

"Of all governments (Mississippi's) is the most miserable and contemptible" a prominent settler wrote. The end result was the region stayed culturally and economically wedded to New Orleans, and most residents tried to ignore the fact that they were a part of Mississippi.

Following the crushing defeat of the British incursion at New Orleans in 1814, the settlers of all heritages saw that they were going to be permanently wedded to the United States and they might as well make the most of it. A federal official who toured the area after the annexation declared the residents "Spanish when sober, violently American when drunk."

Six
The Cracker Culture

In the early 19th century, Southeast Mississippi was a grazier's paradise. Beneath the trees on the uplands was a solid covering of native bluestem grass. The creek bottoms between the hills were thick with a native bamboo that stays green year around and these bottoms also volunteered highly nutritious cool-season annual grasses in the winter. The combination of these two forage resources provided year around grazing for cattle and sheep. Best of all, this grazing resource was free.

While 60 acres of land could be obtained by homesteading it for several years, this was far too small to support the several hundred head of cattle a comfortable living required prior to the Civil War. Also, the fast exhaustion of the soil nitrogen in the stream-side alluvial soils under cultivation made living in one place longer than four or five years untenable. Consequently, the people largely eschewed land ownership and built only rude cabins due to their short tenure in any one place. To outsiders from Natchez or New Orleans, these people appeared poor but most were often far more wealthy than the average cotton planter. They just kept their wealth in four-legged livestock rather than in real estate and slaves.

This whole grass-based eco-system was created and preserved by frequent fire and the grazing of large animals. Without occasional fire, the tender tips of the bamboo quickly grew beyond the reach of the cattle and the hills became covered with hardwood brush called "the rough" that smothered out the grass. The average size settler's herd was around 400 head but the cattle were grazed co-mingled with the cattle of other ranchers in herds of a thousand or more. These large cattle herds typically had an accompanying herd of 500 to 1000 hogs. The cattle provided protection from predators for the hogs and much of the hogs' food supply in their manure.

A visitor to the region in 1817 commented that the region was "peculiarly adapted to the rearing of hogs and cattle; for they require neither salt, nor attention in the winter; and nowhere in the United States are they raised in greater numbers...."

In 1841, J. F. Claiborne noted there was no country "where sheep are so free from disease as in the pine woods." In Southeast Mississippi, it was wool rather than cotton that was the "white gold." And, this would become even more true after the Civil War.

The graziers kept their herds bunched tightly to prevent predation from the many predators, which included wolves, panthers, pumas, mountain lions, jaguars and human rustlers. The whole region was open range and it was the responsibility of landowners to fence livestock out rather than the reverse.

The Longleaf Pine Belt

"The country was one great pasture where large numbers of cattle and sheep fed upon wild grasses that grew among the pines in the spring and summer and upon reeds and canes in the bottoms during the fall and winter. Hardwood and pine mast provided food for swine. There were great numbers of deer, bear, turkeys and squirrels in the woods. Wild game was so plentiful up to the Civil War that the deer had trails in the woods like cattle. All the hunter needed to do was to take a stand behind a tree near the trail and wait for his game...."
Mississippi Harvest-Lumbering in the Longleaf Pine Belt from 1840 - 1915, Nollie W. Hickman

Pannage

Pannage is the fee paid to the landowner for the right to forage with pigs.

Needless to say the manufacture and sale of cypress fence pickets for urban residents was a big business in the region.

One trademark of these graziers was a long leather whip. This whip not only allowed them to get the attention of the cattle with its sharp crack but allowed the grazier to kill poisonous snakes on the ground from horseback. It wasn't long until these graziers began to be called "crackers." This term was widened to include all Southerners by the 19th century.

"Cowpennings," where the year's new calf crop would be branded and the fat steers sorted out for sale, were a communal undertaking and great entertainment for the whole community. At these pennings, the graziers would show off their whip-cracking, horse racing and shooting skills for the ladies.

By 1850, the region that had been Spanish West Florida was producing one million grass finished steers a year. These three- to four-year-old steers sold for between $10 and $12 a head delivered to New Orleans or Mobile. At that time in south Mississippi there were four times as many cattle and hogs as humans and the graziers ruled the roost. No politician would dare suggest that cattle should not be free to roam the region's city streets unmolested.

It typically took 15 days to drive a herd of cattle from Augusta (southeast of present day Hattiesburg) to Mobile (a distance of approximately 60 miles on today's highways). In

Piney Woods

In 1808, Fortescue Cuming reported that the Piney Woods region had a far healthier climate than the lowlands along the Mississippi River but predicted the area would "never draw inhabitants to it while a foot of cane brake land or river bottom" remained in other sections.

addition to cattle and hogs, sheep and turkeys were also driven overland to market in Mobile and New Orleans. In the 1840s, historian J. F. H. Claiborne witnessed a roundup near Leakesville.

> **White Bacon**
> Fried fat back, or white bacon, was served as the main course when meat was in short supply.

"Many of the people here are herdsmen, owning large droves of cattle, surplus increase of which are annually driven to Mobile. These cattle are permitted to run in the range or forest subsisting in summer on the luxuriant grass with which the teeming earth is clothed, and in winter on green rushes or reeds, a tender species of cane that grow in the brakes or thickets in every swamp, hollow and ravine. The herdsmen have pens or stampedes at different points in the forest, where at suitable times they salt the cows, and once or twice a year they are all collected and marked and branded.

"This is a stirring period and quite an incident in the peaceful and somewhat monotonous life of the woodsman. Half a dozen of them assemble, mounted on low built, shaggy, but muscular and hardy horses of that region, and armed with rawhide whips of prodigious size, and sometimes with a catching rope or lasso, plaited of horsehair. They scour the woods in

Whipstock

The ox driver's whip was made of plaited cowhide, eight to twelve feet long. It was mounted on a slender stick six to eight feet in length. This stick was called the "whipstock." The "popper" at the end of the whip was made of dressed deerskin. The long whip made it possible to flick a loafing ox from any position alongside the team. However, the "popper" was primarily for the ox driver's own entertainment. Skilled drivers could make their whips crack like a rifle or boom like a cannon. Ox drivers were paid between $1.25 and $2.00 a day by logging companies.

gallant style, followed by fierce looking dogs; they dash through swamps and morass, deep ravines and swim rivers, sometimes driving a herd of a thousand heads to a pen, or singling out and separating with surprising dexterity a solitary steer which has become incorporated with another herd. In this way cheering each other with loud shouts and making the woods ring with the crack of their long whips and the trampling of the flying cattle, they gallop thirty or forty miles a day and rendevous at night at the stamping ground."

Graziers returning from Mobile after selling their cattle became a prime target of holdup men. One of the worst of these was James Copeland. He and his gang terrorized Southeast Mississippi for nearly a generation. He was finally caught and hung in Augusta in 1857.

The graziers totally disdained the cotton culture with its emphasis on plowing and slaves. "Why would anyone want to be a slave to a bunch of slaves?" they asked. The graziers saw no point in working when their livestock would make their living for them. They thought that anyone who worked when he did not absolutely have to was crazy.

With the animals doing all of the work, the Cracker graziers had plenty of time to pursue what they termed "the sensual pleasures" and produced huge families averaging over 10 children per couple. They also enjoyed hunting, fishing, dancing, drinking, gambling, fighting and just plain loafing.

The Scots brought with them their knowledge of distilling a liquor from almost anything that contained carbohydrates. Area favorites were muscadine grape wine, pear wine, persimmon beer, sweet potato whiskey and "40 rod rum" from cane

1844 Prices

In 1844, in Hancock County, Misssissippi, meat of all kinds sold at retail for 2.5 cents a pound. Fine grade flour sold for $2.50 per barrel. Superfine was $2.75. Sugar was 1.25 cents per pound. Candy cost 2.3 cents per pound.

syrup skimmings. The name 40 rod was said to be the distance you could walk before falling on your face after consuming a cup of it. They also adopted the Indian favorite of corn beer.

Following Celtic tradition, Crackers tried to be as self-sufficient as possible. Much of this self-sufficiency was due to extremely high freight rates of $1.25 to $1.50 for each barrel brought up from the coast. High labor keelboats upon which crews of 12 to 20 men poled up the shallow rivers or "bushwhacked" by pulling on overhanging branches were the only way to get imports from the coast. Cross country, East-West travel was hindered by very high ferry crossing fees at the major rivers so most commerce flowed North and South on the streams and rivers.

The region's trade was primarily salt and biscuit flour in, and hides, cornmeal, dried venison, hams and produce out. The wooden barrel was the primary shipping container for virtually everything and cooperages were a major consumer of red gum and magnolia trees.

Rot resistant cypress was prized for roofing shingles,

Aprons

In the 1800s single women would advertise their sewing talents by embroidering on the outside of their apron pockets. Women who were married had to have their husband's permission to show embroidery work. To avoid conflict, most married women wore pockets on the inside of their aprons.

Marriage Customs

Most people in the interior of Southeast Mississippi were unchurched until the early 20th century and the rise of the evangelical Baptist Church in the region. Holding hands and jumping over a broomstick together in the presence of witnesses served as a legal marriage ceremony in the absence of a minister.

fence pickets, shutters, water barrels and cisterns as cypress imparts no flavor to a liquid held by it. Until the advent of the steam "dry kiln" in the mid-19th century there was little demand for yellow pine lumber due to its sticky resin. Longleaf Pine was prized primarily for ship masts and spars and its tar and pitch were used in sail-powered ships to make the ship's rope rigging and sails resistant to rot.

Live oak was highly prized by the navy for cannonball resistant warship hulls and was the only tree species the government made any effort to protect from illegal harvest. This was seldom a problem as the acorn production of these huge trees for pork production was worth far more than the timber.

Prior to the Civil War, 60% of America's pork was produced from woods-grazed pigs in the South. Hernando De Soto had brought 13 pigs with him from Spain. By the time he reached the Mississippi River his swine herd had reached 700 head despite Indian thefts and his soldiers' consumption. De Soto described America's lower coastal plain as "a garden-like land of fruit bearing trees, among which a horse could be ridden without any trouble." One mature persimmon, mulberry or chestnut tree could carry one hog for the fruiting season.

The Cracker graziers despised trade and "mercenary employments" and preferred to pay their bills with cattle rather than cash. Upon arriving in a new area, they would, following Indian advice, girdle the trees along a creek and let them die. Once they had dried enough to float, they would cut them down and brand each log with their personal brand. When the heavy winter rains came they would roll these logs into the creek and

Rafting

Sending timber to tidewater via rafting was common in Southeast Mississippi. Rafting was possible on any stream having banks four to five feet high where logs could be maneuvered. In almost every locality in the region there was usually one stream where logs could be rafted.

let them float down to the Gulf of Mexico. The coastal saw-mills would gather them and send payment back to the owner of the tree's brand by mail. The fact that the trees that were being cut legally belonged to the federal govern-ment was conveniently ignored by all concerned.

Sawmill Gravy

Sawmill white gravy, made from bacon grease, flour, water and milk was poured over biscuits, or fresh fried tomato slices when they were in season.

The newly cleared alluvial stream bank shelf would then be roughly plowed, often with woven bamboo-fenced pigs, and then planted to corn grown simultaneously with melons and climbing legumes such as peas and beans. Packing the area with multiple crops was an Indian way of utilizing the soil's minimal amount of available nitrogen before it was lost. The corn yield was only about 20 bushels to the acre if grown without a companion legume. In contrast, sweet potatoes would yield 200 to 250 bushels to the acre and quickly became the major carbohydrate feedstuff for both humans and animals.

The other major crop was sugar cane. An acre would yield about 400 to 500 gallons of syrup and provide all the sweetener and rum a family needed. An acre or two of long-staple Sea Island cotton and a few sheep yielded enough home-spun cloth to clothe a family. About the only things people

Cribs And Log Rafts

At the confluence of the creeks with the region's major rivers, individual logs were placed 10 to 15 across and pegged with a hardwood binder across them to form what was called a "crib." Several of these cribs would then be roped together to form a raft. One of these cribs would be designated as the kitchen crib and would carry a full time cook. The rafting journey from Hattiesburg to Moss Point on the Gulf Coast would normally take several weeks.

Cordwood

In the decade of the 1850s, America burned 878.5 million cords of wood for fuel. Selling cordwood was a profitable sideline for pioneer farmers.

bought were salt for curing meat, flour for biscuits, hats, boots, lead and gunpowder. Most stores in the region would accept cattle in lieu of money.

The biggest contribution to the region's cuisine came from the Indians. They introduced the settlers to watermelon, squash, black-eyed peas, velvet beans, sunflowers, corn bread, grits, hominy, bear, alligator, turkey, racoons, opossums and shrimp. They also taught the settlers how to preserve meats with smoke and to fertilize the mineral deficient soils with wood ashes.

Unlike the better soil regions, farmers here did not cluster into villages but stayed widely dispersed and moved frequently. The warm moist winters caused the soil organic matter to quickly burn away under cultivation, and in most instances would only grow two years worth of nitrogen-feeding crops before being totally exhausted. This fast wearing out of the soil was the reason the graziers put very little into their houses and farmsteads as they knew they would soon be abandoned. Yards were kept swept clean to bare dirt as protection from wildfire and the woods immediately surrounding the houses were burned every year to kill ticks and chiggers and to

Wood as Fuel

Prior to the Civil War, wood was the primary fuel of steamboats. A passenger in 1820 reported that the steamboat on which he traveled consumed 128 cubic feet of wood, or one cord, per hour. A standard cord was four feet high, four feet wide and eight feet long. In Southeast Mississippi, steamboat captains would take on what fuel they needed from farmer provided, bank side, wood stocks and leave payment in corn or pork.

drive away snakes.

One common observation of outsiders was how healthy the people in southeast Mississippi were. It was said a doctor would soon starve in the region. The people of New Orleans attributed this good health to the "ozone" or blue

> ## Sawn Lumber
> Prior to the Civil War, sawn lumber in interior Southeast Mississippi was considered too expensive to use for anything beyond the family living room.

haze created by the pine trees. The yellow fever and malaria that so plagued New Orleans was unknown in the Piney Woods until the late 19th century. This was because the people got their water from flowing streams rather than the rainwater cisterns that bred the deadly Malaria mosquito. The Pearl River at Columbia before the Civil War was so clear one could see the bottom in 15 feet of water.

The Cracker graziers were heavily libertarian in their politics. With a crop that could walk to market, the Cracker graziers saw no need for improved roads and bridges and the accompanying taxes and bureaucrats. Most avoided owning land and kept all of their wealth in their herds of livestock. Cattle were not only currency but were the primary means of transport and traction as well. Oxen did almost all of the hauling and plowing. Unlike horses and mules, oxen didn't mind walking through the many stream fords or skidding logs in swampy areas. The training and sale of oxen teams was a major income source as a trained ox would bring four to five times more money than a fattened three-year-old steer.

Also, the fine-grained hide of a five-year-old ox was

> ## Land Rush
> The opening of the Indian lands in north Mississippi to settlement in the 1830s, largely depopulated Southeast Mississippi and ended its nascent experiments with cotton culture.

Mulberry
One mulberry tree can feed one hog for three months.

considered the gold standard for leather and the finest shoe and boot soles were always made from ox hide leather. Did you know that an acre was the measurement of the amount of land an ox could plow in a day? Well now you do.

An ox could work for four hours but then needed two hours of grazing and ruminating before it could work another four hours. Consequently, the people in this area lived on Spanish time with their biggest meal at two in the afternoon followed by a two-hour siesta. The distance between settlements was also set by the ox. An ox could travel seven to eight miles before it needed to stop to graze. Consequently, grist mills and general stores tended to be spaced about seven to eight miles apart. You can still see this "ox-limit" in the close spacing of small towns in Southeast Mississippi.

Whole grains quickly go rancid in hot weather and a weekly visit to the grist mill for fresh corn meal was an essential journey. Almost all bread consumed before the Civil War was cornbread. The type of hard wheat needed for white bread will not grow nor keep in the subtropics. The soft red winter

Guidelines For Finishing A Pig
In America, we consider a pig "killed off the slop" as unfit to eat; and so he is. All our pigs are kept up in a pen, and fattened with Indian corn, or corn meal for several weeks previous to killing. A hundred pounds of corn meal, (mixed with water to about the consistency of very thick mush) is said to be equal in fattening pigs to two hundred pounds of dry-shelled corn. They should be kept up, and well fed for eight weeks; and occasionally, in the country, where such fruits are superabundant, the pigs should have a regale of melons, peaches, and such.
Miss Leslie's New Cookery Book 1857

wheat that would grow in the South could only be used for biscuits, cakes and cookies. Most interior grist mills were only set up for the grinding of corn and most biscuit flour was imported from Mobile or New Orleans in large wooden barrels. The grist mills of the region primarily used turbines

Pig Diets
Pigs love strawberries, blueberries, hazel nuts, hickory nuts, pecans, acorns, roots, bamboo cane, reeds, wild rye and white clover. There is no objectionable smell with pastured pigs.

rather than overshot wheels due to the gentle slope of the land. Most water mills were combination mills that could saw lumber, grind corn and gin cotton. These small water-powered mills dominated Southeast Mississippi until late in the 19th century and many continued into the 20th century.

Hard cheese was unknown in the region because even the winter months were too warm for its aging. Consequently, fresh milk, salted hand-churned butter and its byproduct buttermilk were the primary dairy products. Milk was only available during the green season. Dairy cows were allowed to continue to suckle their calves and were only milked once a day. A sizable percentage of this milk soured before it could be consumed and was fed to household hogs nearing finish along with any table wastes. This sour milk combination was called hog slop. Both hogs and chickens to be harvested were fed table

Guidelines For Eating A Young Pig
The pig should not be more than three weeks old. If not fat, it is unfit to eat. To be in perfection, a suckling pig should be eaten the day it is killed, or its goodness and tenderness is impaired every hour. The custom of roasting a very young pig has now gone into disuse, it being found that baking answers the purpose equally well or better, and is far less troublesome.
Miss Leslie's New Cookery Book 1857

Peanuts

"A pig whose diet is 50 to 70% peanut grows a ham with an incredibly sweet and delicate succulence, which when well-cured, well-cooked will take precedence over any other ham in the world."
Too Many Cooks (1930), Rex Stout

wastes for the last two weeks to "cleanse" their digestive systems of cow manure. Sour milk and cornbread fed chicken was considered to be a gourmet eating event.

With no refrigeration, there was no such thing as leftovers. Every meal had to be created from scratch, and preparing food was an all day activity. The warm weather largely prevented the routine consumption of fresh beef, bison and venison because most of the meat from large animals would spoil before it could be consumed. Consequently, small animals such as chickens, ducks, turkeys, baby pigs, young lambs, baby calves, squirrels and rabbits that could be completely consumed by a family at one meal dominated the meat diet. This was supplemented by salt-preserved beef and pork. Salt for meat and hide preservation was a major import to the region from New Orleans and Mobile.

Spanish breed cattle were the primary cash crop of the region and were driven overland to New Orleans and Mobile for sale. At those two ports, the animals would be slaughtered, the tallow rendered, the hides and meat salted for export to Europe or to the West Indies to feed sugar plantation workers.

Pig Behavior

Pig rooting helps control insect pests, moles and voles. It breaks up the soil, encourages natural mulching and distributes seeds in segmented, cylindrical droppings. Pigs also love to kill snakes. They will toy with a striking snake until it tires and then kill it. They then bury it for several days before eating it.

Until the early 20th century, trade between Southeast Mississippi and the Caribbean was far greater than trade between the region and the northern United States. Pascagoula-born singer, Jimmy Buffett, once noted that he considered the Mississippi Gulf Coast the northernmost point of the Caribbean and trade-wise that was certainly true.

> ## Kudzu
> Kudzu is better for pigs than alfalfa pasture. Pigs once grazed on kudzu for most of the year in the South.

In the 19th century, the hide and the fat of the steer were worth far more than the meat. At that time, factories typically used one large steam engine and distributed its power around the plant with line shafts and pulleys that connected to leather belting. This leather belting created a huge new demand for hides. Also, beef tallow was found to be the only lubricant that would not break down inside the hot cylinders of the steam engine. The demand for tallow for steam lubrication caused pork lard to replace the Scots' preferred beef tallow as the primary frying medium.

The Cracker graziers learned that feeding corn to their grazed pigs before slaughter would "harden the fat" and make a solid, light colored lard. In contrast, the fat of acorn grazed pigs was nearly liquid at room temperatures and dark in color. However, care was taken to not feed so much corn that the pork lost the "wild" acorn flavoring they preferred. Also, corn was always in short supply and was a primary human food staple, so it was closely rationed to both pigs and chickens who were expected to make their own way in the woods until just before harvest. Today, dried hams from acorn-finished pigs sell for

> ## Ham
> A "smithfield" ham could only come from a pig fed peanuts for a year and a day. Peanut finished pork was described as incredibly sweet with a delicate succulence.

Pork

"Pork has an advantage over other meats. Because of the subtle unctuousness of its fat and the sweet blandness of its flesh, it usually tastes better preserved (pickled or salted, smoked or seasoned) than fresh."
Bruce Aidells' Complete Sausage Book

over a thousand dollars a pound in Spain and we now know that the "soft fat" produced by acorns and other fruits is much healthier for you. While smoked and aged hams became prized delicacies in the Appalachian region, a good ham requires alternating periods of warm and very cold weather during the winter curing season. It was the lack of the latter that kept bacon, rather than ham, as the south Mississippi standard until the advent of refrigeration.

Prior to refrigeration, pigs and cattle could only be harvested during the region's infrequent cold snaps. During these cold snaps the meat had to quickly be salted and smoked for preservation. This process required at least three continuous days of cold weather and such long periods of cold weather are

Hints On Heating Ovens And Baking

A heap of wood should be placed in the center of the oven on the brick floor, and then set on fire. While the wood is burning, the door of the oven must be left open. When the wood is all burnt down and reduced to a mass of small red coals, the oven will be very hot. Then shovel out all the coals and sweep the oven floor with a broom, till it is perfectly clean, and entirely free from ashes. For baking bread, the floor of the oven should look red, and a little flour thrown in should burn brown immediately. If you can hold your hand within the mouth of the oven as long as you can distinctly count twenty, the heat is about right.
Miss Leslie's New Cookery Book 1857

rare in the region, thus a lot of meat was ruined by the sudden return of warm weather. Luckily with pork and venison, the cool harvest season coincided with the acorn drop and resulted

19th century Food Measurements

Dry Measure

One pound of 16 ounces of wheat flour is one quart.

One pound two ounces of Indian corn meal is one quart.

One pound one ounce of soft butter is one quart.

One pound of broken up leaf sugar is one quart.

One pound one ounce of powdered white sugar is one quart.

Ten eggs weigh one pound.

Liquid Measure

Four large tablespoons are half a jill.

Eight large tablespoons are one jill.

Two jills are half a pint.

A common-size tumbler holds half a pint.

A common-size wine glass holds about half a jill.

Two pints are one quart.

Four quarts are one gallon.

About 25 drops of any thin liquid will fill a common-sized tea-spoon.

Four table-spoons will generally fill a common-size wine glass.

Four wine-glasses will fill a half pint tumbler or large coffee-cup.

A table-spoonful of salt is about one ounce.

Dry Measure

One half gallon is a quarter of a peck.

One gallon is half a peck.

Two gallons are one peck.

Four gallons are half a bushel.

Eight gallons are one bushel.

Miss Leslie's New Cookery Book 1857

in the harvest of well-fattened, flavorful meat. Such was not the case with grassfed cattle, which reach their prime condition around June 21st when the weather is totally unsuited for an unrefrigerated harvest. Consequently, while people in Southeast Mississippi raised cattle for a livelihood, their personal eating preference was for pork and chicken.

Pigs and chickens are omnivores. This means they can digest both plants and meat. This wider diet makes them much easier to raise and fatten than pure herbivores because they can get concentrated protein and energy by occasionally eating an

Steak Guidelines

The meat of a young well-fed heifer is very good; and that of an old ox (that has done working, and afterwards been fattened well) may be made of superior excellence. The best steaks are those from the tender-loin. Those from the round or rump require beating with a rolling pin. A steak-mallet tears them and destroys the juices of the meat. Without beating they will generally be found to be too tough or hard for an American taste, though much liked in Europe. Do not beat them so much as to tear the meat and exhaust all its juices. We have seen them pounded into dry shreds, scarcely adhering to each other. When first put down, take care not to set it at once too close to the fire, but place it rather more than two feet distant, that the meat may heat gradually. At first, baste the meat as soon as it begins to roast, with a little fresh butter, or fresh dripping from yesterday's beef. Then, when its own fat begins to drip, baste it with that, all the while it is cooking. Gradually move it nearer to the fire, turning the spit round frequently, so that the meat may be cooked equally on all sides. When it is nearly done, sprinkle it slightly with a little salt.

Miss Leslie's New Cookery Book 1857

earthworm, frog or crawfish. It is this animal protein, primarily from insects, that makes free-ranging chicken egg yolks a brillant red orange.

Beef did not become America's preferred meat until the advent of the easy fattening Shorthorn breed in the late 19th century. This English breed was early maturing so that it marbled at a young age. The Shorthorn and later, the Hereford, could produce finely marbled meat solely from grass. Meat protein is practically tasteless and almost all of the flavor in meat is from the fat. Also, it is the fat in the meat that brings a feeling of satiety and fullness. Unfortunately, the fever tick kept this new breed out of the region until the tick was eradicated in the late 1930s. The Spanish heritage, tick-resistant breeds were very slow maturing and poorly muscled but could live solely off the land with no care. Consequently, the shift to the new easy marbling, more flavorful, English breeds was very slow in the region and so was the increase in regional beef consumption.

Lean meats must be cooked at low temperatures to avoid becoming dry and tough. Stews are an excellent way to cook lean meats and were the way most Southeast Mississippians ate beef and game meats. From the Spanish and the Afro-Caribbeans, the Scots-Irish learned that cooking meats with hot

Venison Guidelines

To eat venison in perfection, it should be killed when the deer can find plenty of fresh food in the forest, and when they have fattened on the abundance of wild berries, which they can obtain during the autumn. Buck venison is considered better than the meat of the doe. The haunch, or hind-quarter, is the best part, and the fat upon it should be thick and white. The shoulder, or forequarter, is the next best piece. The haunch should be roasted from three to four hours according to its size.
Miss Leslie's New Cookery Book 1857

peppers, onions and garlic would make them safe to eat even if they had turned a little rancid in the summer heat. As a result, these condiments were always included. A Maine yankee passing through the area in 1846 was not impressed with this style of cooking and said, "They live too well in this country for me. They kill everything with pepper and salt and spice so that you could not tell what the original is. We breakfast at seven, dine at two and sup at six. We eat far too much dinner every day."

By 1861, the value of the hogs, cattle and sheep in the South were double the value of the cotton produced at one half a billion dollars. Unlike the Hollywood version of Southern history, the majority of the wealth of the antebellum South was built on grass and livestock—not cotton and slaves.

Seven
The Salt War

The American Civil War was primarily fought along navigable rivers and railroads because of the huge baggage trains of food and forage the armies required. In Southeast Mississippi, the only railroad near the region skirted the Alabama/Mississippi border, running from Mobile to Meridian and the only truly navigable river was the Pearl and it was only navigable seasonally. Consequently, the shooting War largely passed the region by.

The Confederate government quickly found it could not rely entirely upon volunteers and began a military draft in early 1862, which soon became widely unpopular. In late 1862, the Confederacy withdrew almost all of its troops in Southeast Mississippi to defend its stronghold at Vicksburg. With the troops went any semblance of law and order. For the remainder of the War, Southeast Mississippi became a "no man's land" between Union-held New Orleans and Confederate-held Mobile. This made the region a magnet for army deserters and outlaws.

Some of these deserters organized themselves into paramilitary groups called "Jayhawkers" who preyed upon the unprotected graziers and their herds of cattle. The inability of the Confederate government to maintain law and order spurred even more desertion as terrified wives wrote their husbands about the abuse they were suffering at the hands of the Jayhawkers. By the fall of Vicksburg in July of 1863, the

Appetite Killer

During times when money was scarce, and there was not enough food to eat, it was customary to use a pinch of tobacco or snuff to help kill the appetite.

public's enthusiasm for the War had largely disappeared.

One group of deserters in Jones County verbally allied themselves with the Union and attacked a Confederate recruitment post in Augusta, Mississippi. This triggered a large Confederate response and resulted in the capture and hanging of the group's leaders. During this raid some 1000 Confederate army deserters were caught and returned to service. The Confederate draft agents were totally non-selective and drafted Canadian and British visitors as readily as local residents. By the end of the war, the draftable age ranged from 15 to 75. Most of the management positions in the South were filled by mustered out amputees.

The only major military action in Southeast Mississippi was a Union calvary raid in November of 1864 across the region at approximately the latitude of the future city of Hattiesburg. The military purpose of this raid was to cut the Mobile and Ohio Railroad at Buckatunna, Mississippi, near present-day State Line, Mississippi, and thereby isolate Mobile. The raid was aborted after the Union raiders obtained a copy of the Mobile newspaper which accurately detailed the Union

Cotton Culture

Unlike graziering, cotton culture required good roads for the transport of the heavy cotton bales. Many planters believed that freighting distances of more than ten miles were uneconomical. This tied cotton to the riverbanks before the Civil War. Most antebellum Southern railroads were built to provide inland cotton planters with access to a nearby navigable river and were not designed to provide long distance rail transportation. This greatly limited their strategic usefulness during the Civil War.

attack plans and the thousands of Confederate troops awaiting them. Aborting the raid, the Union Cavalrymen participated in a great "cow-killing" and slaughtered all the livestock they came across during their retreat to the Gulf Coast where ships awaited them. While this was an overt attack on the South's food supply, a much more successful strategy against the Southern food chain was the Union Naval

Sparse Rations In Dixie

In 1864, a Confederate soldier received a monthly allowance of ten pounds of bacon, 26 pounds of coarse meal, seven pounds of flour or hard biscuit, three pounds of rice, one and a half pounds of salt and whatever vegetables were in season.

blockade that President Abraham Lincoln imposed seven days after the firing on Fort Sumter.

While the South was largely self-sufficient in food production, it lacked one major component—salt. In the mid-

1865 Shortages

"The Federal blockade (of the Mississippi coast) was tightened by the use of shallow-drafted gunboats from Ship Island to prevent the coast from obtaining needed food and commodities. As a result, its people suffered great privation. They had no coffee or sugar, they had to tan their own leather. The women often spun cotton or wool to make their own clothes. These shortages were partially alleviated by trading between federal officials and local fishermen on an "off-the-record" basis. Shortages became worse as the war went on. The horses had been taken for the cavalry, and the women had to plow and plant the fields. People cut up felt hats to make soles for shoes, since there was no leather. They parched corn as a substitute for coffee."

Louisiana's Loss, Mississippi's Gain A History of Hancock County, Mississippi, Robert G. Scharff

Beef, Pork and Salt

The primary meat of Union soldiers was beef, both salted and fresh. The salted beef was green in color and much unloved. Union soldiers were willing to trade away their coffee rations for Southern pork.

19th century salt was the primary food preservative for both meat and vegetables. This Achilles Heel had been masked by the ready availability of cheap mined rock salt from England. This salt was used as ballast in English ships coming for cotton. During the French and Spanish colonial periods, salt from evaporation ponds in the Caribbean provided the South's salt. With the Gulf Coast's rainy summers, low-cost salt from evaporated sea water was not possible and the even lower cost English mined salt made domestic salt production in wood-fired boilers unprofitable.

Between 1857 and 1860, 350 tons of British ballast salt were unloaded in New Orleans every day. This was the equivalent of one fourth of Britain's total salt exports to the United States. The cut off of English salt sent all food prices soaring in the South but particularly meat prices. In 1861, a 200-pound sack of Liverpool salt sold at the pier in New Orleans for 50 cents. By January 1863, the price in Confederate-held Savannah

Island Misery

Ship Island, Mississippi, became an infamous prison camp during the Civil War. One quarter of the men imprisoned there died of disease or exposure. One 16-year-old Confederate was shot and killed by a guard for putting a sweet potato on a stove out of turn. Another prisoner was shot for standing up and shaking sand from his blanket. The Gulf Coast's last Confederate fortress of Mobile surrendered three days after General Robert E. Lee in April of 1865. The 3500 Confederate soldiers captured there were imprisoned at Ship Island for a month and then sent home.

was $25 for the same weight of salt. Urban residents were unable to obtain pork at any price and Southerners for the first time began to eat beef in sizable quantities.

> ## Spring Feed
> "To keep meat from spoiling in the Summer, eat it in the Spring."
> *Confederate States Almanac*

To tighten the food noose on the South, the Union made attacking and destroying Southern salt works a major part of its military strategy. "Salt is eminently contraband, because of its use in curing meats, without which armies cannot be subsisted," wrote General William Tecumseh Sherman in 1862.

The South was so desperate for salt that in August of 1862, it made salt workers exempt from the military draft. This and the high prices turned Southern salt production centers into boomtowns complete with professional gamblers and "fancy" ladies. Big money was made smuggling salt into the South from the North and from Europe via the blockade runners. A lot of English salt, which had been low-value ballast before the war, became the primary cargo during the war and was shipped to Mexican ports and then smuggled into the South.

Residents on the Mississippi Gulf Coast soon began to make salt from seawater in wood-fired boilers. This they traded for corn meal with farmers in the hinterland. At one time salt reached an amazing $35 a bushel on the Gulf Coast. Interior graziers started bringing more beef cattle to the undefended

Blockade
The Union blockade of Southern ports utilized 471 ships with 2,455 guns. However, this left the high seas largely undefended and Confederate raiders destroyed much of the North's merchant and fishing fleet during the war. The United States merchant fleet would never recover from the Civil War and would cede most of its ocean-going commerce to Great Britain.

Loss

Of the 210 men who marched off to war from Ocean Springs in 1861 only seven returned. Similar losses were felt all across the coast. Southeast Mississippi had lost a whole generation.

Mississippi coast to avoid both the Confederate draft agents in Mobile and having to take Confederate money for their cattle. These cattle were killed on the beach, the meat packed in brine and smuggled into Union-held New Orleans for gold or sold to coast residents for salt. By the end of the war, even the Confederate government was paying many of its bills with salt due to the low value of its currency.

In the end, the Confederacy collapsed because it could not feed its people. In 1864, a bushel of potatoes cost $25 or 10 times as much as in the North. In March of 1865, Lincoln ordered the Union Army to feed any Southern civilian who would sign a loyalty oath. When General Robert E. Lee surrendered in April of 1865, his soldiers had not had a morsel of food in two days.

Eight

The Railroad Era

For all intents and purposes, the Civil War in Southeast Mississippi ended a year before Appomattox. Laws against trading with the enemy were largely ignored by both sides. The shortage of food and absence of law and order sapped all the patriotism out of the region.

Most residents were relieved when Union forces finally crossed the Pearl River from New Orleans near the end of the war and began to occupy the region because they knew at least they would be fed, which was something the Confederate government could no longer do for them.

Southeast Mississippi largely escaped the worst of the Reconstruction Era excesses because it was predominantly white and deathly poor. For several years an internal war continued as returning Confederate loyalists took their revenge on the "jayhawkers" who had preyed upon their families during the War. While these outlaws were ostensibly Unionists, the Reconstruction government made no attempt to protect them; and, in fact, Union forces in Southeast Mississippi had treated them as Confederate combatants whenever they came across them during the War.

The Southern Homestead Act of 1866 ended cash sales of public lands in five southern states including Mississippi. At that time almost all of Southeast Mississippi was still owned by the federal government. These public lands could only be homesteaded and only by blacks or Union loyalists.

Cane Syrup

One acre of sugar cane typically produced 400 to 500 gallons of farmstead syrup. This syrup normally sold for 35 to 50 cents a gallon. However, its price soared to $1.50 a gallon during the World War I sugar shortage.

Ex-Confederates were excluded. This law had little effect in the region other than to rub salt into the War's wounds as few graziers sought land ownership. Homesteads were limited to only 80 acres, which was far too small to support a family in the poor soils of the region. Military occupation of the region ended in 1870.

On the Mississippi Coast, 30 of the steam sawmills restarted in 1866 and interior settlers began floating logs down the region's streams again. Of course, almost all of these logs were stolen from the federal government, but they always had been.

Water transport of logs was extremely cheap and kept the capital costs low enough that there were many small sawmills on the Gulf Coast. These coastal sawmills could load their sawn lumber onto schooners and sell it in Europe and South America where there was a big demand for it.

By 1870 the North had harvested almost all of its stream bank timber and realized it would have to build railroads to reach the remaining timber stands.

Reunited

The Spanish American War in 1898 dissipated much of the lingering resentment in the South over the Civil War. That year Congress removed the last political disabilities on ex-Confederates and the stunning victories won by the American armed forces created an outburst of nationalism. On the Fourth of July 1898, the band at the Harrison County Courthouse played both "The Star Spangled Banner" and "Dixie" for the first time and Southeast Mississippi emotionally rejoined the Union.

Railroad logging is as expensive as log rafting is cheap. This greatly increased the minimum feasible size of a sawmill. Consequently, Northern lumber interests began to get bigger years before Southerners felt the same pressures. As far as the post-war Southerners were concerned their water borne timber supplies were considered limitless and inexhaustible.

Cairo Syrup

The popularity of cane syrup led to its frequent adulteration with low cost corn syrup. Karo Corn Syrup stole its name from Cairo, Georgia, a town famous for high quality cane syrup. Cairo is pronounced K-row in south Georgia.

However, between 1859 and 1879, America's demand for wood and wood products doubled. This was largely due to the construction of many more railroads. As the saying goes, the iron horse runs on wooden feet. Every mile of track required 3000 wooden crossties and in the 19th century in the humid South most of these had to be replaced every five to seven years. Ditto for all those trestles and bridges. Also, 19th century railroad cars were largely constructed from wood and even coal fired steam engines created a huge demand for wooden mine props and shoring. And, the same thing was happening overseas.

Sweet Potatoes

Often forgotten today, sweet potatoes need to be cured to make them really sweet. After harvest sweet potatoes were placed in black painted curing sheds where the sun was sure to raise the interior temperatures to around 85 degrees. The potatoes were kept in this curing shed for two weeks. The potatoes were then moved to underground storage rooms where the temperature was much cooler. Sweet potatoes will keep for months when kept cool and not moved around a lot.

Tupelo Honey

Honey from tupelo gum trees was a major product in the late 19th century in Southeast Mississippi.

A major customer for Longleaf yellow pine were German railroads which found the durable lumber ideal for car sills. The Gulf Coast's postwar lumber trade was primarily with Cuba, the Caribbean, Mexico, Brazil, Germany, France and Holland. As far as trade was concerned, Southeast Mississippi was still not a part of the Union and there was very little North/South trade until after the turn of the century. This was partly due to the gauge differences between Northern and Southern railroads.

Antebellum railroads south of the Ohio River had been built to a wider gauge of five feet than those in the North, which used the British standard gauge of four feet eight and one half inches, which roughly matched the width of Roman chariots. This gauge difference and the lack of a bridge over the Ohio River made North/South rail shipments very costly and set up an East/West rail shipping pattern that has lasted until modern times.

The Ohio River was finally bridged in 1870 but the adoption of national "standard gauge" did not occur until the mid 1880s when the South narrowed its track to match those of the North. This gauge shift was done on the line across the Gulf Coast in a single day on May 31st 1886. By 4 PM the next day, virtually all of the lines in the United States were of the same standard gauge and a unified rail network existed for the first time.

Southeast Mississippi had gotten its first taste of the

Deflation

The late 19th century was a period of almost constant deflation. Pine lumber which had brought $18 per thousand board feet in 1860 only brought $13 per thousand in 1913.

new railroad era with the construction of the New Orleans, Mobile and Texas Railroad across the Mississippi Gulf Coast beginning in May of 1869.

Molasses

Cane syrup is sometimes called molasses but molasses is the residual by-product of sugar manufacturing and is not nearly as sweet. With cane syrup only the water has been removed. All of the sugar and minerals remain.

The expenditures in constructing this railroad almost singlehandedly dragged the Coast out of its post-war depression. The railroad paid high wages and provided a premium market for bridge timber, hand hewn crossties, vegetables, milk, poultry, fish, wagon hire, fuel wood, sand, shell, and dirt. The golden spike was driven near Chef Menteur Pass, 27 miles east of New Orleans on October 29, 1870. By rail a passenger could travel from New Orleans to Mobile in six hours for only $5.00. This was half the price of the steamboats and a fraction of the time, and the passenger steamboat era quickly came to an end for the Gulf Coast.

The almost constant daytime breeze on the Gulf Coast made a summer home there very desirable to wealthy New Orleanians and the new railroad began morning and evening commuter trains to the city from the Coast. This resulted in a influx of wealthy New Orleanians and transformed the Coast into a predominantly Catholic area very different culturally from the interior of the region. The railroad also ran cheap

White Bread

Brown whole wheat bread was considered only fit for rural bumpkins by urban Southerners in the late 19th century. The urbanites thought the quality of the bread was demonstrated by its whiteness. While this was definitely wrong from a health standpoint, this widely held belief created a huge demand for imported flour from the North.

Crossties

Treated crossties did not come into widespread use in the United States until the 1920s. Hand hewn crossties were a major crop for Southeast Mississippi farmers until then.

excursions each weekend from the city making all stops as far east as Ocean Springs so that the less well-heeled could also get a breath of ocean air. While the Coast was always primarily a summer escape for New Orleanians, the new railroad began to promote the Coast as a winter escape for Northerners. This gave the Coast resorts a "second season" and allowed them to remain open all year for the first time.

With the railroad came white flour and refined sugar imports, which competed with locally grown cornmeal and syrup, but it also brought carloads of mule manure from New Orleans' extensive mule-powered street railroad and the city's many livery stables. A 20 ton carload of mule manure delivered to the Coast sold for only $10 in the 1880s.

This huge supply of inexpensive fertilizer allowed the startup of commercial vegetable farming in Long Beach. Dried shrimp hulls and small "refuse fish" were also used for fertilizer. The nitrogen rich small by-catch fish sold for only $2.00 a

Wood Burning Locomotives

In 1860, there were 4,000 steam locomotives in the United States, of which all but 400 burned wood. By 1870 approximately 10 million cords of wood were consumed by steam locomotives annually. In the South where trains were light and wood was plentiful trains continued to burn wood into at least the 1880s. The last wood burning common carrier railroad in the United States, the Mississippi and Alabama, was in Southeast Mississippi and closed in 1949 without having burned a single lump of coal. A wood burning Shay steam locomotive continued to work in Picayune, Mississippi, into the 1960s.

ton. By-catch fish were also
used to fertilize the huge live
oaks on the coast to stimulate
acorn production for pig
finishing. The huge "Friend-
ship Oak" on the campus of
the University of Southern

> ## Rail Networks
> Railroad mileage in the
> United States increased
> from 30,626 miles in 1860
> to 160,000 miles in 1890.

Mississippi in Long Beach was fertilized by burying by-catch
shark meat near its roots for many years.

Major truck crops grown on the Gulf Coast were radishes, carrots, green beans, celery, shallots, cauliflower, cab-
bage, turnips, beets, okra, peas, tomatoes, watermelons, sweet
potatoes and irrigated rice. Most of the vegetables were sold in
New Orleans and Mobile prior to the building of the Gulf and
Ship Island to Jackson in 1900. The swiftness of the coast-wide
train service also allowed fresh fish and barreled oysters from
the Gulf Coast to be sold in New Orleans for the first time.
Cattle, turkeys and hogs from the interior that formerly had to
be driven overland around Lake Pontchartrain could now be
driven to the Coast and shipped into the city by rail.

Dummy Lines

Logging railroads in Southeast Mississippi were commonly called "Dummy Lines." In the 1870s many subur-
ban horse drawn streetcar lines replaced their animals with
small steam locomotives. The locomotives were disguised
with a boxy wooden exterior built to resemble a horse car
as this was thought to not frighten passing horses.
In addition, their exhaust was muffled so that they ran
without the typical choo-choo sound of a steam locomotive. Consequently, these silent locomotives were called
"dummies." With streetcar electrification in the 1890s,
these small locomotives were sold for next to nothing and
became a low cost favorite for startup logging railroads in
the region.

The Moving Feast

While the Coast was becoming an urbane and sophisticated outpost of New Orleans, the interior of Southeast Mississippi was still firmly stuck in the pre-war pioneer era of graziering and log rafting and all was not well with both industries. Prior to the Civil War there had been some early warning signs that the forest range was being over-grazed near the Gulf Coast. Many of the canebrakes, which provided the winter feed for the cattle were being converted to crop production. Others were being ravaged by too frequent fire and overgrazing. Hogs were particularly destructive because they ate the bamboo's roots.

The first rule of sustainable range management is that the carrying capacity of the range is set by the winter feed resource and not the summer one. While there was plenty of grass on the uplands, the cane that cattle depended upon for winter feed was dwindling away. This caused many graziers in the late 1870s to shift emphasis from beef cattle to wool production as wool wethers could still do well on the over grazed ranges where cattle couldn't. This shift to sheep was accelerated in 1877 when the state cracked down on the illegal harvest of trees from government lands in the interior.

The rise of wool as a major regional crop was welcomed by the cotton factors on the Gulf Coast as it gave them another crop to warehouse, process and market. Wool and railroad tourism gave the Coast economy three distinct eco-

Lard

"Lard or pork fat is about 40% saturated and 48% monosaturated (including moderate amounts of antimicrobial palmitoleic acid) and 12% polyunsaturated. The omega-6/omega-3 ratio will vary depending upon the pig's access to green, leafy forages. Lard is stable and is the preferred fat for frying. When obtained from outdoor pigs, it is an excellent source of vitamin D."
Nourishing Traditions, Sally Fallon

nomic seasons. In the fall and winter trading in cotton was done; in the spring and early summer wool was handled; and in the summer and early fall the tourist dollars were harvested. Tiny Woolmarket

Corn
Southerners believed that yellow corn was only fit for pigs and grew white corn almost exclusively.

became a major wool marketing center because coastwise schooners could get the farthest inland there. The wool was packed into 300 pound packs for shipment to New Orleans. Eventually, the tiny town would handle as much as a half millon pounds of wool a year. Wool from as far as 120 miles inland came to the Gulf Coast for marketing.

It often took these inland farmers six weeks to make the trip in ox team drawn wagons. They returned with their wagons full of flour, cloth and shoes. By the 1880s Waveland had its own woolen mill and was a major producer of wool blankets for the region.

The Gulf Coast had a handful of major resorts prior to the Civil War but due to the shallowness of the Mississippi Sound each resort required an expensive dock 2000 feet long to reach steamboat depth water.

Gulf Coast Native Sheep
Until World War II, the Gulf Coast Native Sheep was the major supplier of raw wool in the South. A landrace breed made up of Spanish and British breeds, these sheep were never given supplemental feeds or treated for internal parasites. Those that survived this non-management became very heat tolerant and resistant to foot rot and internal parasites. The sheep were only rounded up once a year for shearing. Wool color ranged from white to tan to dark brown. Sheep largely replaced beef cattle on southeast Mississippi ranges with the disappearance of the bamboo cane due to over-grazing.

The Great Fire

On the night of October 11, 1893, most of downtown Hattiesburg burned to the ground. The downtown area was rebuilt with locally made brick and these buildings still make up the majority of the city's present day downtown.

With the coming of the railroad, this expense was eliminated and resorts blossomed all along the Gulf Coast. Each resort had its own farm to provide it with fruit, vegetables, poultry, eggs and dairy products. Cows were milked three times a day for fresh milk and cream cheese and butter were also made daily. A pen of hogs utilized the resort's table scraps. During the summer months, much of the dairy production was fed to the hogs as it frequently went sour before it could be consumed.

Orchards of satsuma oranges, pears, peaches, pomegranates, figs and grapes decorated the resort grounds and provided fresh fruit and jams. In the 1870s commercial pecan orchards started being planted on the Gulf Coast with the new larger Russell "paper shelled" pecans that had been developed in Ocean Springs a favorite. The railroad also allowed the marketing of great piles of fish in the fall of the year to New

Sullivan Kilrain Fight

In August of 1899, two steam locomotives pulling 19 passenger cars brought a rowdy crowd of several hundred New Orleans fight fans to the tiny sawmill town of Richburg just outside of Hattiesburg. There John L. Sullivan and Jake Kilrain fought a 75 round bare knuckle fight for the World Championship. Sullivan won but was arrested after the fight because bare knuckle fighting had been outlawed in the United States. Sullivan was allowed to serve out his sentence from a rocking chair on the front porch of the Richburg General Store where he entertained tourists with tales of his fighting career.

Orleans. Barrels of oysters in their shells were also a major export during the cooler months of the year. In the 19th century, Biloxi was the only place in the country where peeled shrimp were canned.

In Bay St. Louis there was a huge 90 acre vineyard of scuppernong grapes from which a popular wine called Scuppernong Champagne was made. This Champagne was renown for its "medicinal" qualities and it was shipped as far as Chicago and New York. Biloxi-canned figs became a staple in all of the Pullman Palace Car Company dining cars. Fruit, fig and vegetable canning was a way of utilizing the infrastructure of the shrimp and oyster canners during the hottest months of the year when the seafood harvest was suspended.

The railroad allowed the easy importation from the Mississippi River docks in New Orleans of Minnesota hard red wheat flour for bread and Tennessee soft red wheat for biscuits, cakes and cookies. This led to the rise of bakeries all along the Gulf Coast. In Biloxi, Mississippi's first flour mill was opened in 1893 and Southeast Mississippi farmers had their first flour market for locally produced soft red wheat. Prior to the opening of this mill, wheat had been grown primarily as a winter grazing forage in the region.

Prior to the coming of the railroad, locally made cane syrup and honey had been the two major sweeteners. Now, the Coast was flooded with inexpensive refined white sugar which was consumed in huge quantities in the late 19th century. One of

Dinner For A Dime

During the 1880s, excursion trains from New Orleans made a 20 minute stop in Bay St. Louis so that the passengers could buy refreshments from a restaurant in the station. A Negro, dressed as a chef, met arriving trains beating vigorously on a dish pan and announcing "dinner is served." The "dinner" was thin ham sandwiches that cost a dime each.

Beachfront Line

Not content with owning just the steam powered, Gulf and Ship Island Railroad, Joseph T. Jones built an electric interurban railroad from Biloxi to Pass Christian in 1909. The beachfront line hauled passengers during the day and freight at night.

the Coast's major uses for the sugar was for locally made sodas, sarsparilla and root beers. Soda fountains provided women with a social space similar to what saloons provided men. Slightly inland, the cheap sugar stoked the fires of the nascent illegal whiskey industry.

In 1876, the federal government removed the prohibition on the sale of government lands in Mississippi and the sale price was set at $1.25 an acre. This set off a flurry of speculation as wealthy Northerners flocked in to buy land by the tens of thousands of acres as the timber was worth many times the initial sales price. This land buying did not cause a lot of concern among the local residents because: one, they were assured their free grazing would not be interfered with by state law; and two, harvesting the timber would require huge amounts of capital for railroads because the graziers had already stolen most of the timber that could be inexpensively moved by water. A timber survey of Southeast Mississippi in 1876 found that almost all harvest size trees within four miles of a sizable stream had already been cut. This finding is what caused the crackdown on illegal tree cutting in 1877.

It is hard for us today to understand the antipathy the

Water Mills

As late as 1870 there were 16,562 water wheels producing 327,000 horsepower, compared with 11,204 steam engines turning out 314,000 horsepower in the United States.
Many small mills in Southeast Mississippi continued to use water power until the early 20th century.

19th century graziers had toward pine trees. While hardwoods at least provided a mast crop that could fatten their hogs and turkeys, the graziers felt pine trees just stole sunlight and water that could be far better used for growing grass. Consequently, they welcomed the tree removal. This same attitude extended to the state government who taxed standing timber annually the same as a cotton crop. This encouraged timberland owners to cut their trees as quickly and completely as possible.

> ## Radishes
> With the completion of the Gulf and Ship Island Railroad in 1900, Long Beach radishes became the standard bar food snack in Chicago.

The common belief in the American lumber industry in the 19th century was that trees were a one-time crop and could not economically be regrown. The business model was to build mills cheap, depreciate them fast, cut the trees and abandon the land. While the timber companies found the local graziers to be a hospitable people when they were cutting the pine trees, they would find them to be a serious enemy when they tried to regrow them in the 1930s.

In 1880, a railroad started building southward from Meridian, Mississippi, toward New Orleans. This railroad, the New Orleans and Northeastern, would transform the interior of Southeast Mississippi as dramatically as the line across the Coast had ten years before. The railroad construction suddenly

> ## Progress
> The electrification of New Orleans street railways in 1893 allowed Biloxi entrepreneur, E. G. Burkin, to buy New Orleans' discarded mule cars and light rail for a song and build Biloxi's first street railway. In that same year, Burkin put in the city's first telephone service and built its first electric light plant. In true Southeast Mississippi tradition, the electric plant's boilers were fired with wood.

Freeze

A prolonged freeze in 1895 ended the Gulf Coast's tropical citrus industry.

created a huge cash market for food, oxen, labor and hand hewn crossties. Railroad wages were three times the going rate of the Gulf Coast sawmills and quickly created a labor shortage in the region. The construction crews also consumed huge amounts of liquor and their, and subsequent railroad construction crews' rowdy behavior became a major catalyst for the local prohibition movement. By 1900 there were 53 large mills between Meridian and New Orleans and two-thirds of the population in Southeast Mississippi had become dependent upon lumbering for a living.

The New Orleans and Northeastern reached New Orleans in 1883 and was bought by British investors in that same year. Instrumental in building the railroad was an ex-Confederate Colonel named William H. Hardy. While survey-ing the line prior to its construction, he had laid a ruler on a map between the deep water port of Ship Island off the Gulf Coast and Jackson and saw where it would cross the New Orleans and Northeastern line and kept this site in the back of his mind.

After the completion of the NO and NE Railroad, he knew that a northward running railroad would have to skirt the steep hills of present day Lamar County by running along the flat flood plain of the Leaf River near the tiny village of Gordonsville. Consequently, he became a major landowner and

Road Trip

In June 1908 Biloxi seafood tycoon W. K. M. Dukate took his family on the first automobile journey ever attempted between Biloxi and Hattiesburg. The 80 mile journey required a day and a half to Hattiesburg and a full day to return. The 160 mile round trip burned an amazing 66 gallons of gas.

promoter of the town he renamed Hattiesburg after his wife Hattie in 1884. Hardy constructed a large "eating house" adjacent to the tracks where train passengers could be quickly fed while the steam engine took on coal and water. Hattiesburg was an ideal spot for this service as it was roughly halfway between New

Mediterranean Coast

In the 1880s, the Gulf Coast became ethnically even more Mediterranean with arrival of Italian, Greek and Dalmatian immigrants to join with the French and Spanish descended original inhabitants.

Orleans and Meridian. This halfway location caused it to be chosen as a division point with an engine servicing center complete with a roundhouse and turntable. However, one railroad did not a city make and the booming Hattiesburg of Hardy's dreams did not develop.

In the late 1890s Colonel Hardy teamed up with wealthy Pennsylvania oil tycoon, Joseph T. Jones, to build a railroad from the Gulf Coast to Jackson. This railroad was named The Gulf and Ship Island and reached Hattiesburg in 1896. Just as he envisioned, the two lines crossed in the middle of downtown Hattiesburg and was quickly joined by two other railroads). One of these lines ran to Mobile and the other to Natchez where it connected to lines to Dallas and the West. All four lines met in the downtown area. Hattiesburg's sobriquet became "The Railroad Hub of South Mississippi" and it was soon the fastest growing city in the state and quickly became the marketing and commercial center of the Piney Woods lumber industry.

Rabies

Fear of rabies was high during the hot weather months in Southeast Mississippi. The town Marshall of Bay St. Louis warned in the 1880s that "All dogs running at large between the first day of July and the last day of October, shall be by the marshal destroyed without notice."

The Moving Feast

Meanwhile on the Coast end of the railroad, Jones pushed the state legislature into incorporating a "bed of sand with a few shacks, two streets and a creek running through it" into the city of Gulfport in 1898. When the government refused to dredge a channel from the docks Jones had built in Gulfport to deep water at Ship Island, he financed the project out of his own pocket. By 1907, just nine years after its incorporation, Gulfport had become the world's leading exporter of yellow pine lumber and the largest city in Southeast Mississippi.

However, over in Biloxi a new manufacturing plant had been built that would dramatically change the food culture of the region. Southeast Mississippi was about to enter "The Ice Age."

Nine
The Ice Age

In the interior of Southeast Mississippi, foods were preserved by salting, spicing, smoking, pickling and drying as late as the 1890s. Milk had to be consumed soon after it came from the cow and was drunk warm. Fresh meat was only available a few days a year as were fresh fruits and vegetables. This all changed around 1895 as the region moved into the "Ice Age" of mechanically produced ice.

Prior to the 1890s, ice had been an incredibly expensive luxury item in Southeast Mississippi. Cut from northern rivers and lakes, huge ice blocks were shipped down the Mississippi River by steamboats and stored in New Orleans in heavily insulated "ice houses" for warm season sale and use. Some of this ice found its way to the tony resorts on the Mississippi Gulf Coast via steamboat and schooner, but for most of the region ice was something that occurred on a handful of days in the winter and was certainly unknown during the sizzling summer.

Mechanical refrigeration had been invented in Florida by Dr. John Gorrie in 1851 to cool Yellow Fever patients, but it found little commercial application until the 1870s. In 1879, there were only 35 mechanical ice plants in the whole United States. What spurred the adoption of mechanical ice were growing health problems from natural ice cut from sewage-tainted waters. By the late 1870s, consumer demand for "sanitary ice" from ground water spurred the creation of a new industry.

Ice Cream Freezer

Ice cream was produced in small batch, hand cranked churns until 1926 when the continuous process freezer was invented.

One of the first cities to have an artificial ice plant was New Orleans in 1867 but this pioneering plant had few followers for many years due to the high price charged for the ice. There were only 35 commercial ice plants in the United States in 1879 but 200 just 10 years later and 2000 plants 20 years after that. This rapid expansion in manufacturing capacity quickly dropped the price of ice to where virtually everyone could afford it. And, with cheap ice came the "Ice Box."

Ice boxes were typically made of wood, lined with tin or zinc and insulated with sawdust or seaweed. Beneath the box was a pan that collected the melted water from the ice and had to be emptied daily. Horse drawn ice wagons patrolled the city streets looking for houses with "Ice Today" signs in their windows. If you went out of town, you had to leave your house unlocked so the ice man could have access to your ice box to keep your stored food from ruining.

With an ice box you didn't have to worry about your fresh beef going rancid or your milk going sour in the summer weather. Now, you could have leftovers and didn't have to shop daily. The coming of the ice box more than anything else severed humankind from the hand-to-mouth agriculture they had known for centuries. For the first time urban people could be totally severed from the production of their food supply.

Ice changed the processing and transportation of food as

Ice Cream Churn

The hand cranked ice cream churn was patented in 1843. This produced a smoother ice cream and did it quicker than the pot freezer, which was hand-turned back and forth in a bucket of salted ice.

well. In 1867, J.B. Sutherland of Detroit, Michigan, patented the first ice cooled refrigerated railcar. This was first used to bring strawberries from southern Illinois to Chicago, but its use soon expanded into all foodstuffs. In 1888, Armour Meats railed ice-cooled Mid-

> ## Soda Fountains
> Soda fountains replaced bars and saloons as the socially accepted social center in the late 19th century.

western beef from Chicago to Florida for the first time. Just one year later in 1889, New York City residents could buy California fruit that had been hanging on the tree just 12 days before.

Mechanical refrigeration also totally changed the meat packing industry. Now, animals could be harvested and processed year around and not just during cold weather. This allowed beef cattle to be properly "finished" on green grass, and well fattened beef began to slowly replace pork as the number one meat. With its network of railroads running to every corner of the United States, Chicago became the meat packing center of the whole country.

Taking advantage of seasonal climatic differences, cattle could be shipped live to Chicago by rail whenever they were properly finished. Regardless of the weather they could be harvested and cut into primals and these shipped by refrigerated railcar all over the country. To balance the seasonal supply, cattle started to be finished on corn and corn silage during the winter months but were grass-finished during the green season until the end of World War II. Thanks to ice and the refrigerator car, by 1895 the New Magnolia Hotel in Pass Christian could boast that "all of its meats came from Chicago." And, by 1913,

Sodas, Sundaes, Cones
The ice cream soda was invented in 1874 and the ice cream sundae in 1890. The world's first ice cream cones were served at the 1904 St. Louis World's Fair.

Pecans

A pecan boom began in Jackson County in the 1870s as new varieties of grafted pecans became available for the first time.

America's 100,000 refrigerator cars were rapidly reshaping American agriculture from one that supplied local needs to one where farmers concentrated on growing a few crops well and buying in their food supplies just like urban people.

Cheap ice came to Southeast Mississippi in the summer of 1894. The Gulf Coast had several small ice manufacturers by 1893. These small plants largely supplied the resorts, saloons and soda fountain parlors that used lots of ice. The rest was primarily used to cool fish and oysters headed for New Orleans. One of these plants was the Biloxi Hygeia Ice Works that had been built by Charles McCormack, a salesman of the De La Vergne Company of New York, which was one of the pioneer manufacturers of ice making machinery. This plant had its own artesian well for a sanitary water supply, a small electric light plant, and a rail siding for the shipment of large blocks of ice to customers along the coast-running Louisville and Nashville Railroad.

The other ice plant was the Biloxi Artesian Ice Manufacturing Co. This company was the first ice plant on the Coast and was established in 1887 with a small five ton per day ice

Luggers And Schooners

The two fishing boat workhorses of Biloxi were the two-man lugger and the six-man schooner. Both were built broad of beam and with a shallow draft that would allow them to work the shallow waters of the Mississippi Sound and Louisiana coast. During the hot summer months when the seafood harvest was halted for health concerns, the fishermen turned to racing as a diversion. Beginning in 1888 each factory pitted its fastest schooner and best sailors against its rivals for glory, $100, and a keg of beer.

making capacity. This expanded to 22 tons a day in the summer of 1894 due to the demand from local canning plants and fresh seafood marketers. This huge increase in manufacturing capacity collapsed the price of ice on the Coast and so far exceeded the

Green Beans

The green bean was the first vegetable shipped from Long Beach in 1884. By the mid-1920s the city was knows as "the radish capital of America."

local demand that ice was shipped by rail all along the Coast and into New Orleans and where it found a ready market.

There had been some limited use of ice to keep shrimp fresh in the late 1860s but the high cost of imported ice had limited this. The advent of cheap ice quickly found use in the seafood industry. Large ice boxes on local schooners allowed them to stay at sea far longer than had been previously possible, and small scale ice making machines on steam-powered trawlers allowed the harvest of seafood from the largely untapped fisheries of the Yucatan. The combination of ice and railroads quickly created a major seafood boom on the Gulf Coast with fresh oysters and shrimp finding their way into the major interior cities for the first time.

The cheap ice greatly expanded the marketing area for Gulf Coast fresh seafood, and it soon was sold as far away as Birmingham. With completion of the Gulf and Ship Island

Bohemians

In 1890, a Biloxi packing house imported the first group of Polish workers from Baltimore, Maryland, to work the shrimp and oyster seasons. Called Bohemians by the locals, the women and children picked shrimp while the men shucked oysters. For 40 years these Maryland Poles preferred to go back to Maryland for the hot summer months when seafood was not being harvested and most never became permanent residents.

Washing Machines

General Electric invented a small "household" electric motor that could run a washing machine in 1913. Prior to this motor, the company's emphasis had been exclusively on large industrial size motors.

Railroad to Jackson where it connected with the Chicago-based Illinois Central in 1900, iced fresh oysters from Biloxi set off an "oyster house" boom in Chicago. The railroads responded to this new demand for fresh iced seafood with new high speed freight cars that could be hauled by passenger trains in 1900. By 1930 there were 3264 of these "express cars" in service and the Mississippi Gulf Coast became a seafood and winter vegetable adjunct to the city of Chicago.

By 1896 Biloxi was the largest city between Mobile and New Orleans with the city's new found prosperity being driven by five large seafood canning factories. Oysters were the primary product but the two month shrimp season in the spring and a similar season in the fall also added to the bounty. Biloxi fishing boats were capable of harvesting either oysters or shrimp depending upon the season. In 1903, Biloxi passed Baltimore in seafood production and claimed the title of "The Seafood Capital of the World."

The third major technology that would reshape the economy of the United States occurred almost simultaneously as the "Ice Age." This was the coming of commercially pro-

Dalmation Immigrants

Dalmatia, which later became a part of Yugoslavia, had a coast line that very much resembled that of the Mississippi Gulf Coast. During the seafood boom of the 1880s, immigrants from that country to the Gulf Coast became a flood. Immigration authorities in New York soon learned to place a tag on the clothes of all Dalmatian immigrants advising railroad conductors to route them to Biloxi.

duced electricity. In the 1890s, its primary use was to run streetcars and interurban railroads. These urban railroads began to sell electricity to line-side businesses and homes for illumination as an

Saenger Air Cooled
The first "air conditioned" building in Hattiesburg was the Saenger Movie Theater in 1929.

adjunct enterprise. This helped amortize their investment in the power generation plant as traction demand for electricity fell at night when fewer people used the streetcars.

By 1910, Hattiesburg, Pascagoula, and Biloxi had electric streetcars, and electric interurban railways connected Biloxi with Gulfport and Pass Christian, and Laurel with Ellisville. In the sawmill towns, the sawmills often provided electricity as a service to their workers' homes. However, most rural Mississippians would have to wait until the late 1930s and New Deal Rural Electrification to enjoy electric light in their homes.

In 1893, the World's Columbian Exposition in Chicago featured the first "all-electric" kitchen with an electric coffee maker, waffle iron and stove. While electric appliances were technically possible they found few takers. One, people in the 19th century had a strong distrust of electricity and considered it "unnatural." Two, pioneer electric appliances were expensive and notoriously short-lived. For example, ceiling fan motors only lasted a tenth as long as today's. And three, the streetcar companies were not really interested in promoting anything that increased daytime use of electricity. It was not until after World War One when streetcar use began to decline due to the rise of the automobile that the streetcar companies began to aggressively sell electric appliances to homeowners.

Five Cent Flickers
Movies came to the Gulf Coast for the first time in 1900 with "five cent flickers" at Biloxi's Dukate Theater.

The Moving Feast

In 1920, the Frigidaire electric refrigerator became available. However, this appliance was priced considerably higher than a brand new Model T and found few customers. Over the next 20 years, the price of electric refrigerators and electricity would fall dramatically but for most homeowners in Southeast Mississippi, the "Ice Age" of home refrigeration would last until after World War Two.

Ten
The Great Experiment

The Scots-Irish settlers of Southeast Mississippi were heavy consumers of alcohol in all forms. Corn whiskey was used to wash down a meal similar to the way we use iced tea today, and public drunkenness was common. The railroad building era at the turn of the century in Southeast Mississippi was particularly rowdy with open prostitution and numerous bars and saloons. This rowdiness may have been tolerable in the largely male world of the frontier but by the turn of the 19th century people were settling in, marrying and raising families and they were no longer willing to have their wives verbally and physically assaulted on the street by a drunk. Consequently, people began to be receptive to the idea of prohibition. Or should I say, receptive to the idea of prohibition for *other* people. And in the South, the other people they most wanted alcohol denied to were African Americans.

The idea of prohibition, or "the great experiment," was spearheaded by the Methodist Church as early as the 1840s. The Methodists were among the first to make women's concerns a major part of their evangelism and males' heavy drinking was a major concern. Following the Civil War, the prohibitionist theme was picked up by other evangelical churches including the Southern Baptists and Presbyterians.

On the other side were Roman Catholics, Episcopalians and German Lutherans who did not think the government had the right to define moral issues. Consequently, the first "local

Rock And Roll

According to *The Rolling Stone Illustrated History of Rock and Roll* the very first rock and roll record was recorded in the Hattiesburg train depot on July 20, 1936 by the "Mississippi Jook Band."

option" prohibition of the early 1900s split along religious affiliation lines with the predominantly Protestant counties in the interior voting themselves dry and the predominantly Catholic counties along the Gulf Coast and the Mississippi River remaining resolutely wet. This regional ignoring of the prohibition laws did not change when the state voted itself dry statewide in 1908. However, even in interior Southeast Mississippi those who wanted to drink could, as "wet" Louisiana was just a short train ride away.

At that time there was a daily "shoppers' train" that ran from Hattiesburg to New Orleans every morning with an early evening return. This train seldom had over two coaches six days a week but on Sundays the train would require as many as a dozen coaches to satisfy all the people who wanted to ride.

Of course, only a few made it all the way to New Orleans as most got off in Pearl River, Louisiana, the first

Boogie Woogie

Some lumber companies tried to enforce prohibition in their remote logging camps but many found that selling illegal whiskey and providing prostitutes on Saturday night to their workers helped keep them at the camp and provided a highly profitable side venture. In these camps a boxcar was used as a barroom, which featured an upright piano. A style of piano playing featuring a fast pounding bass beat developed that became known as "Boogie-Woogie." Jelly Roll Morton of Hattiesburg was a pioneer popularizer of this style of piano playing. In the 1950s, Jerry Lee Lewis introduced it to a wider audience.

village across the Pearl River, which served as the state line. These thirsty Mississippians would then proceed to drink themselves into a belligerent mob that terrified the local citizenry. This earned the village the ironic sobriquet of "Peaceful Pearl."

Another favorite drinking spot was the floating Blue Goose saloon that was tethered to a tree in Louisiana across the Pearl River from Gainesville, Mississippi. Ringing a provided bell quickly brought a rowboat from the saloon to pick up patrons on the Mississippi side. The proprietor of the saloon reportedly left a huge fortune in cash in the Bank of Picayune when he died.

The prohibition laws also sparked a huge expansion in the manufacture of illegal whiskey called "shinny"or moonshine. During the sugar rationing of World War One, Southeast Mississippi moonshiners bid the price of locally made cane syrup to a record high of $1.50 a gallon. At this rate one acre of sugar cane made into syrup earned more than a year's work in a sawmill. The early move to prohibition in Mississippi allowed both the moonshine makers and the smugglers several years head-start on perfecting their craft before national prohibition was voted into being in 1919. When Chicago mobster Al

Coast Boom

In 1925, a new paved highway across the Mississippi Coast set off a real estate boom that saw many new hotels and resorts built. One of these was the $2 million Edgewater Gulf Hotel in Biloxi.

Isle Of Caprice

In 1923, Biloxi's Buena Vista Hotel built a gambling casino on an island beyond the 12 mile limit off the Mississippi Coast. The casino thrived for nine years but visitors picked the sea oats that held the island's sand together and the casino sank beneath the waves like Atlantis.

The Moving Feast

Capone needed a volume supplier for his 10,000 "speakeasies" he found it ready made in Southeast Mississippi in the tiny village of Kiln, which could literally supply illegal whiskey in railcar volumes.

With hundreds of trained turpentine distillers in the area, the Kiln area rapidly became the center of illegal whisky manufacturing in the region. One small grocery store in Kiln bought 4,000 pounds of sugar a week during the 1920s whiskey boom. Many railcars headed north on the Mississippi Southern Railroad with just enough pine lumber to hide the shipment of whisky inside.

The Mississippi Coast with its many inland running small rivers and bays was ideal for "rum-running." Many sail-powered oyster and shrimp schooners quickly were fitted with gasoline motors so they could participate in the lucrative trade that was winked at by the local law enforcement.

After one massive haul of illegal whiskey, federal agents, rather than smashing the bottles as usual, just dumped them into the Mississippi Sound. Enterprising shrimpers dredged up enough of the whiskey to collapse whiskey prices on the Gulf Coast for several weeks.

By 1920, the Mississippi Coast had outstripped both the Canadian border and the East Coast as an entry point for illegal whiskey with an annual haul of $1.5 million. As in Kiln, the rails were put to use for volume purchasers. In 1924 a routine safety inspection in Biloxi found 1000 cases of whiskey camouflaged by a loose covering of ground oyster shells way-billed as chicken grit.

Just Buying Bullets

The Gulfport police captured four armed men sitting in an idling car in front of a bank and charged them with attempted bank robbery. The men were released when they explained they were just buying bullets before an evening of rum-running.

The Great Experiment

While the repeal of national prohibition in 1933 ended the easy money of whisky smuggling in Southeast Mississippi, Kiln "white lightning" would remain a favorite brand on the south side of Chicago until the late 1940s.

Eleven
The Tragedy Of
The Commons

The United States as a whole slipped into a major economic recession in 1920. The end of the "Great War" in late 1918 ended the war's demand on the economy and sent hundreds of thousands of mustered out soldiers home to unemployment. In Southeast Mississippi, 1920 marked the start of a twenty-year-long severe economic depression.

The vast virgin forest that had fueled forty years of economic boom was almost gone by 1920. State law at the time taxed standing timber annually as if it were a cotton crop. This was because dominant North Mississippi politicians wanted the Mississippi Delta cleared of timber as rapidly as possible and converted to high dollar cotton production. However, this clear-cut policy made absolutely no sense in poor soil, Southeast Mississippi where timber should have been nurtured as a continuous yield crop with the state taxes paid on the timber at harvest rather than annually. Also, the state in a populist frenzy, raised the taxes on the large south Mississippi mills, which helped to discourage a more sustainable harvest.

Due to Mississippi's tax policy, it was in the mill owners' economic self-interest to cut the timber as fast as possible to avoid taxes. Trees too small for economic use were cut anyway just to avoid paying taxes on them. By 1920, most of Southeast Mississippi resembled the grass covered plains of Kansas with not a single tree in sight, albeit littered with thousands of tree stumps.

Acorns

The average oak tree in Southeast Mississippi produces 1000 pounds of acorns a year. Pigs grow one-third faster on acorns than they do on corn.

The large scale sawmills typically ran at full tilt until the last tree they owned was gone, and then they would suddenly shut down. These mills were not only the major source of employment but also provided the electricity for their adjacent mill towns, most of the housing, the local transportation on their feeder railroads, and the town's food staples through their commissaries. Since many of these mills were fully depreciated, their owners often just walked away and abandoned them to the tax collector. As late as the 1960s, many small towns in Southeast Mississippi still had a giant ghostly mill standing in their town center with its rust-colored smokestacks soaring above the surrounding landscape.

Frequently, the adjacent mill town completely died and became a ghost town. Railroad engineers said a nighttime run across Southeast Mississippi in the 1930s really gave them the creeps with its many ghost towns. They called the region "voodoo land." It was like a neutron bomb had hit the region, evaporating its population but leaving the buildings standing.

The Mississippi Gulf Coast largely missed the 1920s depression by concentrating on seafood, whiskey smuggling, real estate speculation, and tourism. Hattiesburg and Laurel survived by converting to value-added timber products such as

Turkeys And Ducks

Domestic turkeys were used by farmers in the Depression to control tobacco hornworms and grasshoppers. Ducks ate grass, aquatic weeds, algae, slugs, eels, leeches, worms, snails, crustaceans and insects. They also help control mosquitoes and beetle larvae.

Pork And Peanuts

The increased yield of a crop grown behind peanuts that had been grazed out by hogs increased enough to pay for the peanut crop. In other words, the pork gain was free.

industrial turpentine from pine stumps, Masonite from saw mill waste and creosote treated poles and pilings. However, the major economic question in interior Southeast Mississippi at that time was what to do with the cutover land?

Some of the large landowners promoted the sale of their cutover lands to unsuspecting Northern farmers with considerable initial success. However, most of these snowbirds returned home after their first dismal crop and the rest left after their second crop failure. There was some success with cotton on the alluvial shelves along the rivers and streams but the arrival of the boll weevil early in 1909 largely put an end to cotton production in Southeast Mississippi where the winter temperatures were too warm to reduce the weevil numbers. Vegetable production and cane syrup were profitable, but only on the alluvial soils, and then only for a year or two. Putting the land back to timber was seen as too long-term of an option to be economically feasible and the free-ranging hogs and sheep prevented longleaf pine seedlings from naturally regenerating.

For the vast majority of the upland region, the only large scale viable crop in the 1920s that people could see was grass. Consequently, the region that had been known as the Piney Woods prior to 1920 become known as the "cow coun-

Pellagra

In the early 1900s 100,000 Southerners died of pellagra from eating too much corn in their diet. The Indians had avoided this disease by always soaking their corn in wood ashes before eating. This process made the niacin in the corn available and prevented the deadly disease.

Stumps

In 1920, stumping and fencing an acre of land in Southeast Mississippi cost $25. After 1920, the Hercules Powder Company of Hattiesburg removed stumps for free.

ties" after 1920 as beef cattle numbers soared.

Keep in mind, the whole region in the early 1920s was open range, even the cities. This meant that grazing was free for the taking and it was the responsibility of landowners to fence the free-ranging cattle out of their yards rather than for livestock owners to fence cattle in. The inevitable result of this situation was an economic conundrum known as "the tragedy of the commons."

In any situation where there is a free, exploitable resource but no restriction on the number of exploiters, there is an economic incentive to maximize the use of the resource in the short-term even if it destroys the resource in the long-term. And, that is exactly what happened in Southeast Mississippi.

Few farmers ever fully understand the basic principles of sustainable livestock grazing. The first principle is that overgrazing is a function of time rather than severity.

This means that you can have 500 steers graze an acre of grass into the ground in just a few hours and not hurt the grass *as long as* the grass has time to fully recover from the

Commercial Fertilizer

Just prior to World War One, German scientists Fritz Haber and Karl Bosch find a process to produce commercial nitrogen for munitions thereby making Germany independent from the need to import Chilean saltpeter. In the 1930s American farmers begin to use commercial nitrogen for fertilizer for the first time. Today, American farmers use 400% more commercial nitrogen than in 1940.

grazing. Grass plants have enough reserves in their roots to recover from a periodic severe grazing or burning by fire. However, if this grazing is too frequent these root reserves become exhausted and the grass will die.

In the 1850s, range cattle in Southeast Mississippi were kept bunched by the herders to prevent predator attacks from bears and large cats. Today, this is called high stock density grazing. This tight bunching caused severe short-term overgrazing but this grass was normally not re-grazed for several years and so had plenty of time to recover. Also, this bunching concentrated the manure and urine and made it more effective as a fertilizer. This is a very sustainable system and could have gone on forever. However in the 20th century, cattle were just turned out onto the range and their grazing was not managed. As cattle numbers increased, the grasses were grazed more frequently and had less and less time to recover.

The second major principle of sustainable livestock grazing is that the carrying capacity of the range in a year around grazing situation is set by the winter grazing resource and not the summer grazing resource.

What made livestock production so profitable in Southeast Mississippi was the presence of the year around green bamboo cane that made winter hay feeding unnecessary. This cane needed both alluvial soils and open sun to grow. Normally, the native cane was the fourth crop in a three-year

Wandering Cows

Until July 30, 1920, cows could wander freely on the streets of Bay St. Louis. Many families had a cow for milk and allowed them to graze freely about the city. These cows soon became "educated" as to how gate latches and bolts worked and many private gardens were destroyed. While urban residents argued for a stock law for many years, few politicians in Mississippi were willing to risk their job over a cow.

Movie Eggs

During the Depression, movie admission in Hattiesburg could be paid in eggs.

cropping rotation because the abandoned land was ideally prepped for the cane to move in. In fact, canebrakes were frequently called "oldfields" because they tended to grow on abandoned farmlands in river bottoms. The dense stands of cane tended to slow the winter and spring floods and cause the water to drop its sediment load in the canebrake thereby hastening the soil's rejuvenation.

As livestock numbers grew, a huge imbalance between the upland summer grazing resources of the region and the lowland canebreak winter grazing resources developed. It didn't matter that there was plenty of un-grazed grass in July if the cattle had nothing to eat in January. The combination of cattle grazing the bamboo regrowth and their companion pigs eating the roots of the plant eliminated most of the canebreaks forcing cattle owners to start making and feeding hay.

The third major principle of sustainable livestock grazing is that the profitability of any grazing enterprise is primarily determined by the amount of hay you have to feed.

By the mid-1920s Southeast Mississippi graziers were having to feed a lot of hay and the profitability of cattle raising

Home Deliveries

During the 1930s, home delivery became a big item. In addition to bread, milk and ice, New Orleans stores delivered customers' purchases on the Gulf Coast by truck. Gulfport Laundry picked up and delivered its customers' laundry weekly and Standard Coffee company delivered its products direct to homes. In Bay St. Louis, one of the daughters of the Taconi family delivered hot stuffed crabs by bicycle to the purchaser.

Poultry

In 1910, 88 percent of America's chickens were in flocks of less than 80 hens.

plummeted. And, there were other problems as well.

The cattle tick prevented the rail transport of Southern cattle to the new national terminal markets in the Midwest during the warm weather months. It was said that just the sight of Southern cattle would cause Northern cattle to fall dead in their tracks. While the native Southern cattle were genetically resistant to the tick, these cattle were generally poorly muscled and slow to mature and fatten. With the advent of the railroad refrigerator car, Southern graziers found their highest priced local markets were increasingly buying well-fattened carcasses from the Midwest, which were more tender and flavorful. Also, the advent of reliable small electric motors was sending the old central engine and leather belt system of industrial power to the scrap yard, and the demand for industrial belting leather, which had been the economic underpinning of Southern cattle production, was in sharp decline.

In the mid-1920s a South-wide program was adopted requiring all cattle owners to dip their cattle periodically for the fever tick. While this program was designed to increase the marketability of Southern cattle it was seen by many Southern

Dairying

In 1935, milk in Southeast Mississippi brought $1.50 per hundred pounds of milk. The hauling cost was twenty cents a hundred, and the cottonseed meal used to supplement the cow's grazing cost sixty cents a hundred. This left a profit of seventy cents for each hundred pounds of milk sold. Due to such high profits, dairying became a major industry in Southeast Mississippi during the Depression.

Chickens

In the 1930s, chickens were sold live. It was killed and dressed by the store's butcher for the customer.

cattlemen as "government meddling," and a covert war was launched against the tick eradication program. This war included the dynamiting of the government-built dipping vats. In 1926 Mississippi made an attempt to end open-range grazing. This created such a howl of protest that it was quickly modified to a county-option program. This left most of Southeast Mississippi still in open range, but the range was quickly closed in the more urban and cropping oriented counties.

All of these beef cattle difficulties resulted in many Southeast Mississippi graziers switching to wooled sheep as their primary enterprise. Wool had always been a major product of the region but it had always taken a back seat to beef production. Now, in the 1920s it was wool's turn in the driver's seat.

Wool is primarily produced from castrated male sheep called wethers. In Southeast Mississippi, these wool wethers were only sheared once a year in the late spring. The native sheep of the region were naturally parasite and heat resistant and could thrive on a range that would starve a cow to death. Actually, the wool quality is better if a sheep is slightly underfed, so they were seen as the ideal replacement for cattle on the region's ravaged ranges. By the end of the 1920s, it was re-

Fever Tick Restrictions

Due to fever tick restrictions, Southern cattle had to be harvested immediately upon arrival in the North and could not be fattened prior to slaughter. Consequently, they could only be used for canned beef and received a very low price. Tick restrictions also caused Southern hides to sell for half the price of Northern hides. The fever tick was considered eradicated from the South in 1943.

Troop Movements

In 1941, the movement of one Army division from Camp Shelby required the dispatch of a 17 car passenger train (15 cars and two kitchen cars) every four hours for 25 days.

ported that there were five million sheep in the 60 miles between Hattiesburg and Gulfport and one whole city block in Gulfport was taken up by wool marketers. If cotton was the "white gold" of North Mississippi, wool was the "white gold" of Southeast Mississippi.

Unfortunately, wool and cotton are made into cloth and clothing is a deferrable expenditure during tough times. When the cotton market collapsed in 1929, wool went with it. In 1933 most of the sheep in Southeast Mississippi were driven to Gulfport, loaded onto ships and sold to Mexico.

The one expenditure that wasn't deferrable regardless of the economy was food, and food production became the economic salvation of the region during the 1930s.

Due to the dependence upon free grazing on the open range, few farmers in Southeast Mississippi owned over forty acres. Therefore, New Deal extension efforts were on enterprises that produced a lot of dollars per acre. These included dairying, pears, pecans, peaches and satsuma oranges.

"An investment in a pecan orchard, together with a small dairy herd or flock of chickens, or both, and a few pigs—there you have a pleasant occupation that will maintain your interest in life and living, and a job from which no one can

Camp Shelby

In 1940, 12,623 workers reopened Camp Shelby for Army use. Hattiesburg's population doubled to 40,000 during World War II, becomes famous as a place for "food and females," and acquires what was termed a "garish seediness."

'fire' you because your step has lost its elasticity, or your hair is turning to silver," crowed a 1933 New Deal brochure for Southeast Mississippi.

Traditional crops such sweet potatoes, green beans, turnips, cabbages, radishes and other vegetables were coupled with new canning plants that widened the marketing area and increased the availability of local food to year around. A large scale industrial turpentine factory in Hattiesburg cleared Southeast Mississippi's farmers' land of stumps to obtain the stumps for distilling. Farmers rushed to take advantage of this as stump clearing was a hard and thankless task that deterred most farmers from vegetable farming and putting in improved pastures. Picayune boasted the world's largest strawberry field at over 1000 acres and shipped out 200 carloads of satsuma oranges in 1931. Also, a large steam syrup mill was built in Picayune to increase the quality and production of cane syrup in the area. War in Asia in the late 1930s cut off the world's primary Tung oil supply and sent prices in Tung-rich Southeast Mississippi soaring.

With the fever tick under control, easier-to-fatten breeds of cattle came into the region. These new breeds coupled with an emphasis on high-gaining winter annual forages created an interest in local beef production again. The heat-tolerant Jersey cow and the wide-spread ownership of ice boxes that could keep milk cool created a dairy industry in the region for the first time.

In 1936, the Hattiesburg trade area of 180,000 people included 28,000 full-time farmers. By concentrating on things people ate, they earned five times the income of cotton farmers in North Mississippi and 25 percent more than the urban

---

Rice

In 1942, James L. Crump, a retired New Orleans cotton broker, bought 3800 acres of Jourdan River bottomland and raised upland rice on it for the next 15 years.

Fishing Boats

In 1932, the last sail powered fishing boat in Biloxi was motorized.

workers of the region. Getting in the spirit, the University of Southern Mississippi in Hattiesburg plowed up its golf course and allowed students to work off their tuition producing food for the cafeteria. In 1940, the average distance food traveled before its was consumed was only forty miles. This distance would compress even further during World War II when forty percent of the nation's vegetables were produced in backyard "Victory Gardens."

Even forestry changed from an emphasis on big mills and volume to one of small mills and value. Rather than concentrating on high volume/low value export "squares,"or minimally sawed large logs, the surviving smaller mills focused on loom spindles, broomsticks, kegs, boxes, pressure treated poles and piling and wooden furniture that husbanded the small amount of remaining mature forest. However, such small scale manufacturing would soon find a new competitor for the region's forestry resources.

In the early 1930s, G. H. Tomlinson invented the recovery boiler, which greatly lowered the cost of making kraft paper by allowing the recapture and reuse of the expensive

Office Of Sheriff

While Mississippi was a legally dry state until 1966, the state collected more than two and half million dollars in "black-market tax" on the sales of illegal liquor annually. There was no state prohibition agency and Federal law officers just winked at the law. The office of sheriff was based upon the fee system. This made him both the chief enforcement officer, and quite often, the county's major liquor dealer.

Eggs

In 1950, Americans ate 400 eggs a year versus 235 today.

inorganic pulping chemicals. Unbleached brown paper made from immature Southern pine trees could be used to make a very sturdy linerboard that could then be used to make shipping boxes that were much lighter and less expensive that the wooden boxes commonly used. This new highly profitable papermaking process created the first corporate interest in reforesting the vast cutover lands of the Southeast, which could often be purchased for the back taxes.

Since the papermakers could use immature trees, they soon saw that fast growing species of pine trees could be "farmed" just like a cotton crop. Unfortunately, these new fast growing species were highly susceptible to fire in their early years and, of course, faced the two major seedling pine predators of free-ranging hogs and sheep. The low wool prices of the Depression pretty well eliminated the sheep, and the foresters realized the best way to eliminate the hogs was to eliminate their food supply of mast producing hardwood trees on their lands. Consequently, the corporate "tree farms" were converted into huge monocultures of nothing but pine trees.

Local graziers took this cutting of the hardwoods as a huge attack on their livelihood and retaliated by burning the new pine plantings when they were most vulnerable to fire. Often they would leave a sign that read, "You've got the money, we've got the time. You cut the hardwoods. We'll burn the pine."

While cattle grazing was pretty much left alone, these graziers realized that without periodic fire the grazing resource

Milk

In 1945, the Navy base in Gulfport consumed 4,000 quarts of milk every day.

would revert to what they called "the rough" and would be a jungle of brush and briars that would offer little to nothing for a cow to live on. Consequently, they signed up for the covert war on "paperwood" plantations as well.

The paper companies enlisted the New Dealers in a propaganda war against the local graziers saying they were holding back "progress." Most of the foresters in the Forest Service were from the West where total fire exclusion was the prescribed course of action. They didn't realize that the Southeastern forests actually required periodic burning to retain a pine culture. In the end, a modification on the total fire exclusion policy came about because of the lobbying of wealthy Northern quail hunters who saw that fire was necessary for quail survival on their Southern hunting plantations.

While open range grazing lasted in some areas of Southeast Mississippi into the 1960s, there remained a continuing animosity between the college-trained corporate and government foresters and the indigenous graziers. This animosity spilled over into government propaganda tracts that insinuated that anything "old" in agriculture was wrongheaded and unscientific, and this attitude spilled over into foods as well.

After World War II, a lot of Southerners saw the indigenous local foods that they had eaten throughout the Depression and the war as "poverty foods." Sweet potato consumption plummeted from 31 pounds per capita in 1920 to just four pounds in the 1960s. This attitude was egged on by national brand name advertising on television. Soon artificial Tang became "better" than fresh squeezed orange juice and a Twinkie better than anything Mother could produce at home. Young people were primed for a McDonald's Restaurant by years of television advertising before one ever came to their community.

Hominy Grits
Corn flakes are just flat rolled hominy grits.

The Tragedy Of The Commons

The combination of the invention of the refrigerated truck in 1949 and the Interstate Highway system in the 1950s put an end to the "Wall of Distance" that had protected small local farmers from large-scale ones using subsidized irrigation water and cheap Mexican labor in the West. Little by little local food agriculture died.

Cattle were still raised but were shipped to the Midwest for finishing and then the meat shipped back for consumption. Eggs came from a confinement hen house rather than your backyard. Pork production, which had been the centerpiece of southern agriculture for 200 years, similarly disappeared into a confinement house in Iowa.

Today, the vast majority of young people in Southeast Mississippi have never met a full-time farmer.

Chapter Twelve
Lessons From Our Heritage,
Visions For The Future

In researching this book, there were a lot of new things I learned even after 33 years as the editor of an agricultural publication. One of the biggest things I learned was that the problems of production agriculture were the same as today but people found solutions to these problems without the use of petroleum or other outside purchased inputs. I wish we could rekindle that pioneer spirit in Southeast Mississippi. Here are some lessons I think we need to relearn from our forefathers.

1.) Feeding the family from the farm was the first priority of their agriculture. Making money was secondary.

2.) Crop farming was limited to the alluvial bottom-lands. The upland areas were reserved for grazing and forestry.

3.) The cropping sequence was planned to reflect the decline in soil nitrogen.

4.) The cropping sequence did not exceed three years.

5.) Pastured animals were moved frequently to fresh pasture, which avoided overgrazing and kept animal performance and health high.

6.) Fruit and nuts from tree crops made up a large portion of both human and animal diets. (Pecans, pears, persimmons, peaches, and acorns.)

7.) The use of pigs, ducks and geese minimized labor for weed and pest control.

8.) Low crop yields were offset by direct harvest of the

crop with animals. (Hogged down corn)

    9.) Free ranging poultry provided fly and tick control.

    10.) Animal parasites were controlled through land rotation and the mixing of animal species. (Most parasites are species specific. For example, sheep and cattle break each other's parasite cycle by serving as a dead-end host for the parasite.)

    11.) They concentrated on crops that lent themselves to inexpensive long-term storage and a longer marketing window. (Sweet potatoes and corn.)

    12.) They hedged bets against weather extremes with short maturity corn, co-planting of nitrogen feeders and legumes, wide plant spacings and crops that covered the ground with rain softening vines.

    13.) They used tough land-race plant and animal genetics that needed no crutches or band-aids to survive.

    14.) They periodically used agricultural fire for mineral recycling, brush control and forage refreshment.

    15.) They used wood ashes both as a mineral fertilizer and as a livestock mineral supplement.

    Farming is about capturing and using things that are free and not about buying inputs and machinery to beat Nature over the head with. It is also about adding as much value as possible to whatever solar collector you choose before you sell it. If you ignore either on these two basic tenets, farming will be much less profitable than it could be.

A Vision For The Uplands...
Landscape As An Economic Development Tool

    As you have read, the first Europeans who arrived in Southeast Mississippi were not greeted by a dense, forbidding jungle of trees and underbrush such as exists in our region today. In contrast, it was a beautiful open savannah of wide spaced trees and grass created by agricultural fire and bison grazing. A planned return to such a beautiful landscape could have a major economic impact upon the upland hills of our region from both tourism and agriculture and forestry.

Condé Nast Traveler had an interesting report on the new discipline known as environmental psychology. Researchers in this field have found that viewing open green landscapes has a profound impact on both our mental and physical health. Stephen and Rachel Kaplan, professors and researchers at the University of Michigan in Ann Arbor, found that urban workers denied a view of a rural landscape became "irritable, erratic, and less competent." Conversely, hospital patients recovering from surgery who could see a green landscape from their window needed fewer drugs, complained less, recuperated more quickly, and were discharged from the hospital sooner.

A pastoral landscape that combines open grassland with wide-spaced trees and a glimpse of water was found to be the universal landscape ideal. This was true of seaside dwellers, New York urbanites, South Korean rice farmers, and Africans living in tropical rain forests. In fact, so universal was the love of this landscape that some researchers believe it may be genetic in origin. They believe a DNA memory of the African savanna is carried deep within every human being. It was in this landscape that early man found living most easy and free of stress.

Laboratory experiments have found that urban and rural dwellers report they feel happier and less fearful when looking at a photograph of such a landscape. In contrast, pictures of tight spaced, dark, jungly forests choked with undergrowth and pictures of swamps induced stressful feelings. For forests to be seen as stress-relieving they had to be of the widely spaced open montane-type.

French Agritourism
Landscape subsidization is found in France where agritourism is seen as the last best hope for economic renewal in their rural areas.

Another pleasing landscape derived from the savanna is that of water and palm trees on a clean open beach. The Japanese Zen garden, the English landscape and the American city park are all attempts to recreate the restful savanna look. Looking at a savanna creates a feeling that is reported as "relaxed awareness"—a natural high.

These psychological findings about landscape are thought to have major significance for both tourism and real estate. Environmental psychologists suggest that travel may in fact be a search for a more preferred landscape. Tourism-dependent Switzerland has known this for years and has long provided massive subsidies to farmers willing to maintain an open, pastoral landscape in its mountains. The UK is also re-gearing its agricultural subsidies into "landscape" items such as rebuilding stone walls and re-establishing hedgerows rather than supporting commodity production.

People do not like broad stretches of any kind of sole use landscape as it quickly becomes monotonous. The French are trying to create a jumbled tapestry of small fields and pastures interspersed with small, non-threatening patches of forest. Their research shows it is this varied, busy landscape that attracts urban weekend tourists to the countryside where they will buy the artisan food production of their small farms and non-industrial hand crafts.

While urban farmers' markets bring the countryside to urban consumers, the French want to bring their urban consumers to the countryside. There they would spend the weekend in small inns and hotels and keep the farmhouse restaurants full. Other rural entertainments such as horseback riding, canoeing and rafting would be provided. While it sounds Disneyesque,

Open Land

The amount of open land in Mississippi has decreased by two million acres since 1915. Now we have roughly the same amount of forested land here as we did in 1890.

this is an idea that the urban French taxpayer likes and is willing to pay for.

An unexpected effect of this approach in France has been a re-population of rural areas by urban runaways. Today, half of all French farmers have lived in the cities at one time or another in their lives. And, the rise in high value artisanal agriculture has largely come from these well educated, business-savvy newcomers.

A 2005 survey by the University of Vermont found that 96% of that state's visitors said scenery was a "very important" to "important" reason for visiting.

Eighty-four percent said that seeing cows and farms was valuable.

Fifty-nine percent said they would not revisit the region if all the pastoral farms went away.

This is a very important finding as tourism is a $1.46 billion dollar business in Vermont and is why the state of Vermont now subsidizes the preservation of pasture in their state. Vermont and New England as a whole are rapidly nearing total reforestation.

All of this has implications for Southeast Mississippi and the whole Southeast. I know people from other regions driving across the almost totally forested landscape of the Southeast report feeling claustrophobic and depressed. I know I have felt the travel tedium produced by the almost totally forested landscape between Hattiesburg and the Gulf Coast. Unfortunately, this unloved landscape is growing.

Auburn University said the long harvest cycle of single-use industrial forestry cannot support a land-based rural

Working Landscapes

A University of Vermont survey reported that tourists liked what they termed "working landscapes." These are the landscapes produced by people supporting themselves by pastoral farming.

economy. This is a primary reason 36 of Mississippi's 82 counties have a smaller population today than they had in 1940.

Unfortunately, the Mississippi Department of Economic Development currently sees total industrial forestation in these struggling rural counties as an economic goal rather than something to be resisted. Their view is that the one thing we can grow cheaper than anyone else is a pine tree. While this may be true, it is a poor economic choice if one only gets a paycheck once a lifetime.

However, I don't intend to knock forestry. What I propose is a hybrid forestation that reflects our region's heritage and that can both maintain cash flow better and produce a dramatically better-looking rural landscape that can enhance our growing tourism and travel-oriented economy.

Recent research at LSU's Hill Farm Research Station in Homer, Louisiana, indicates that re-integrating grazing and timber management can greatly benefit timber growth and total economic return.

"In business time is money," explained Forestry Project Leader Terry Clason. "This is particularly true in a long-cycle crop like forestry. Being able to grow a sawlog in 25 years versus 35 years tremendously lowers opportunity costs."

Clason said the biggest growth limiter to a pine tree was another pine tree. "You have to keep the forest canopy open to produce fast tree growth but when you do that the understory vegetation is stimulated as well. This can be a big problem or it can be a big opportunity if grazing is incorporated."

Grazing In The Pines

Grazing beef cattle and sheep in the pine barrens of the Southeast dates back to Colonial times. The traditional open range system consisted of un-managed cows and un-managed pine trees. Costs were low but so were returns. Stocking rates were frequently in the 40-acres-to-a-cow range.

He said traditional forestry management plants 680 trees per acre. Trees are then subsequently thinned as they grow. This tight spacing is used to create a barren forest floor and promote natural pruning as the trees drop their shaded lower limbs. Clason said this system creates three problems: a slow growing tree, loose knots that can weaken the wood's strength and virtually no high-value clearwood. On the March 1998 pine timber market, regular saw logs were bringing around $550 per thousand board feet. However, clearwood—knotfree wood used for veneer and architectural trim and millwork—was bringing $800 to $900 per thousand board feet. Clason said the New Zealand system of forestry is designed to maximize the creation of high value clearwood through hand pruning.

"Once we make the decision to hand-prune, we can spread the trees out and go for maximum timber growth as well. Once we spread the trees out we find that an acre of timberland can support virtually the same stocking rate of livestock as an open pasture. It's a win-win situation."

Clason recommends that trees initially be planted in rows 24 feet apart and with six to eight feet between the trees in the row. This is 300 trees per acre. If a planting contractor is used, the cost will run around $300 per acre. The wide rows not only provide for excellent grazing but for subsequent easy logging machinery access.

Cattle and timber prices run on different economic cycles and can therefore both complement and subsidize one another during the down phases of their cycles. During reces-

Tree Planting Costs

Opportunity cost is the income foregone by not putting the money spent on a production activity into a financial instrument. This is usually figured at an eight percent rate per annum. At this rate the opportunity cost doubles every nine years. In a 30 year period a $300 planting expense for trees compounds to over $2400.

sions, saw timber demand can virtually disappear but trees can be "stored on the stump" until economic recovery as long as the forest owner has an alternative income source. Beef, as a food, is not hurt as badly as timber during economic cycles but has its own down cycles due to periodic overproduction.

Clason said hand pruning should start when the trees are eight to ten feet tall. They should be pruned again after an additional eight to ten feet of growth and can be pruned a third time if a very large sawlog is desired.

"The beauty of this to a cattleman is that all the forestry work can be done when there is nothing else to do. Adding forestry can help keep hired labor fully employed year around."

Once the trees reach eight inches in diameter, 200 of the trees should be removed as paperwood or chip-and-saw. This will usually occur at age 10. The wide rows and lack of lower limbs greatly facilitate this thinning. At 11 to 13 inches, or 10 to 15 years of age, he recommends the landowner take out half the remaining trees and leave 50 trees per acre to grow to high value saw timber. Timber income will just about equal harvesting costs until this point. It is only at this point the big profit phase from forestry begins.

At age 25 to 30, Clason said one can clearcut or take half and leave half for another five years depending upon market conditions. "At today's clearwood prices a fast growing big tree is really increasing in value fast." More and more foresters are seeing the value of allowing mature stands to grow

Cattle And Timber

A major benefit of adding cattle to a timber operation is that many of the agronomic practices required for the trees can be charged against the cattle operation. This allows them to be expensed immediately rather than carried forward as a basis against future forestry income. This not only saves taxes on current cattle income but lowers the opportunity cost basis of the timber as well.

to really big trees before harvesting. This extends the "savannah landscape" effect and the maximum productivity of the pasture beneath the trees as well.

In yet one more example of wholistic serendipity, large pine trees have been found to respond exceptionally well to the pasture's fertilization program, particularly to nitrogen. Clason said they have seen growth increases of as much as 30% on nitrogen fertilized pastures compared to legume based pastures. "At $45 to $50 more tree growth per year, the increase in tree growth almost completely pays for the pasture fertilization program."

Clason said on today's open market the final harvest grosses between $6000 and $8000 per acre. This is a net of $2400 to $4000 over average land and direct opportunity costs.

He said this return could be greatly increased by delivering one's trees to the mills rather than selling them on the stump. In other words, direct marketing logs just like vegetables from a market garden. He said he has mentally mapped out a five employee, 5000 acre production system of staggered age tree plantings that on today's beef and timber markets could produce a thousand 800 lb yearling steers and 1,500,000 board feet every year. On today's beef and lumber markets that is around $1,500,000 in annual gross income. Taking these animals to grass finish at 1200 pounds would up this combined income to $2,000,000 a year.

"We have an opportunity here to create an economic system that is not economically exploitive but regenerative," Clason said. "Managing our resources more intensively can

High Stock Densities

Using high stock densities in timber stands there is no need for frequent fire to recycle the pine straw since the cattle's cloven feet mash it into the ground. Currently, smoke from agricultural fires is one of the largest sources of atmospheric CO_2 pollution.

create more jobs in our communities, more income for the landowner and a beautiful park-like landscape. It's really a win-win system for everyone."

A Vision For The Lowlands...
A Return To The Movable Feast

Over the last ten years, my wife and I have struggled to grow an organic garden in upland soils in Southeast Mississippi. This is not something I would recommend. Our upland soils are best kept in grass and trees. While a much smaller percentage of our land area, our alluvial lowlands offer more promise but only if we realize that cropping in a subtropical climate cannot be done organically for longer than three years due to the exhaustion of the soil's nitrogen.

While most people think bugs would be the major problem in our naturally buggy climate, we have found this to not be the case. Maintaining soil nitrogen is the major problem. Due to our warm winters, open soils burn away their organic matter year around. A study in Arkansas found that this organic matter burn per acre was equal to the amount of coal a small steam traction engine would burn in the same amount of time.

While small gardens can offset this with frequent imports of purchased manure and compost, the best solution to this problem on a commercial scale is to return to a planned land rotation between pasture and crops similar to what the Indians and the pioneers did a hundred and fifty years ago.

When I first saw the Argentine pasture/crop land rotation twenty years ago I knew I had seen the future of commercial organic agriculture. Their five/three rotation was five years

Pasture/Crop Rotation

The beauty of a pasture/crop rotation system is that almost all the major weeds of crops are excellent forages, and virtually all the weeds of pasture (thistles) are easily controlled with tillage.

in leguminous pasture followed by one year of corn, followed by winter wheat, sunflowers or soybeans. This rotation allows the crops to be grown with no artificial nitrogen and a minimum of other inputs including tillage for weed control.

Where this system really shines is when the cropping phase is used to produce high value food crops rather than commodities. A good place to see this land rotation system in use with high value crops is at Homestead Heritage Farm in Elm Mott, Texas, near Waco.

Homestead Heritage is a sustainable living community of nearly 900 people who primarily support themselves by growing and selling high-value foodstuffs and handmade wooden craft items such as violins, guitars and fine furniture. The community teaches economic self-sufficiency through frequent schools and the families grow most of their own vegetables in personal gardens. They also maintain small flocks of personal poultry for eggs and meat.

The centerpiece farm is 510 acres, which includes 48 homesteads with about 250 residents. The primary emphasis of the farm is to feed the community and only surplus items are sold to the general public. The farm is organic in practice but is not USDA Certified Organic. Foodstuffs sold include grassfed beef products, cheese, sorghum syrup, stone ground grits, corn meal and wood fired bakery products.

The base farm is divided between a stony upland plateau and a 60 acre alluvial valley adjacent to the Brazos River. These two soil groups are separated by a sheer rock cliff that

Animal Traction

At Homestead Heritage, all tillage is done on the alluvial soil with home-raised oxen, horses and mules. The decision to use animal traction was made by the community's founders to maximize labor and minimize purchased inputs. This policy is described as keeping the farm at a "human scale."

drops over 100 feet. The upland area is mostly grazed with goats and sheep and is not tilled. Dairy cows graze the temporary lowland pastures.

The land rotation is currently two years of alfalfa pasture, followed by one year of corn or sorghum, one year of wheat or oats and one year of sweet potatoes, peanuts or Southern peas (also called cowpeas or black-eyed peas) or Black beans. A shorter pasture sequence than Argentina's hurts the crop yield but a high yield per acre is not a primary management goal. Cash flow is.

The crop sequence reflects the decline in soil nitrogen over the three year growing period with heavy nitrogen feeders planted first. What surprised me was the growing of sweet potatoes, a nitrogen feeder, in the last year of the rotation. Butch Tindell, the director of education at Homestead Heritage, said sweet potatoes liked a soil that was both sandy and only moderately fertile. If you have too much nitrogen, the sweet potato just grows a lot of vine rather than a bigger tuber.

While sweet potatoes may be last in the rotation it is first in profitability with a gross dollar production of between $20,000 and $40,000 an acre at retail. This compares with corn at $4500 an acre, sweet sorghum at $3500 an acre and wheat at $2500 an acre. These are the retail prices worked backwards to the land. For example, the wheat produces 1920 pounds of whole wheat flour sold for $1.30 a pound.

What makes sweet potatoes so profitable is that they

Pigs As Harvesters

Pork from pigs finished on a combination of sweet potatoes and peanuts were considered the ultimate eating experience in the 19th century South. Hogs are especially useful with sweet potatoes and peanuts because a sizable percentage of these crops is always unintentionally left in the ground at harvest and the pigs will happily harvest these while plowing the field for the next crop.

require minimal processing compared to corn or wheat. However, minimal processing doesn't mean doing nothing to add value to the product. For example, the sweet potatoes are "cured" for two weeks in a high humidity root cellar kept at 85 degrees. Then the temperature is dropped with ventilation to around 60 degrees. This hot, moist curing raises and fixes the sugar level in the potato and makes it much sweeter than uncured supermarket sweet potatoes. Prior to World War II, Southerners ate a whopping 31 pounds of sweet potatoes per person per year. Today, they eat only four to five pounds so there is a lot of "heritage" market share to recover.

Historically the South offset its lower yields with direct animal harvest. As late as World War II, the majority of the South's corn crop was "hogged down" rather than mechanically harvested. The corn, wheat, cowpeas sequence was what farmers in the Waco area (and most of the South) grew 100 years ago and it still works.

The Homestead corn is milled into grits and corn meal using a modern Meadows Mill stone mill from North Carolina. In contrast, the wheat is ground into flour by water wheel driven, French-cut stones from the 18th century.

Grits are the larger pieces of corn from the milling process and corn meal and corn flour are the smaller corn particles. These three products are separated in a mechanical sifter as all three result from a single grinding. Corn meal is used for cornbread, hush puppies and muffins while corn flour is used for pancakes, muffins, doughnuts and breadings for fried meat and chicken. Homestead Heritage's primary corn product is coarse milled grits. These large particle grits have

Stone Ground Corn

Stone grinding produces a nutty flavor with a pleasant texture. The low temperatures produced by the slow turning stone prevents the wheat germ from oxidizing and the heat destruction of the vitamins in the grain.

become extremely popular with top Dallas chefs and they wait in line to get them.

Wheat products are determined by the type of wheat grown. Traditionally in the South and lower Midwest, soft red winter wheat was grown and in the West and western upper Midwest, hard red spring wheat was grown. Soft red wheat makes crumbly products such as cookies, cakes and muffins. This is because there isn't enough gluten (protein) in soft red wheat to hold the end product together. In contrast, hard red wheat with its higher gluten will hold together and so is used for bread. Interestingly, Homestead Heritage grows a Russian variety of winter hard red wheat that defies tradition and allows Homestead to produce high value bread products from their home-raised winter wheat.

Wheat bread is relatively new in the South. Southerners traditionally ate un-leavened corn bread and biscuits because yeast was very expensive and didn't keep well in the hot climate. In contrast, biscuits were not widely eaten in the North until the Kentucky Fried Chicken franchise popularized them there.

The other major arable crop is sweet sorghum for syrup. In the early 20th century, there were 20 million gallons of sorghum syrup produced annually in the United States. Today, there are less than a million gallons produced. Butch said in Southeast Mississippi to go with sugar cane as the yield is much higher and the skill required to make a quality syrup is much lower.

Interestingly, it is easier to produce a sweeter flavored

White And Yellow Corn

In the 19th century South, humans exclusively ate white corn and considered yellow corn only fit for swine. White corn was called the "poor man's rice" as rice was the upper class carbohydrate of choice in Dixie. Only in the western parts of Texas was yellow corn eaten in the South.

syrup organically than with commercial fertilizers. Butch said too much readily available nitrogen from either manure or commercial sources will cause a salty off-flavor in the syrup.

Homestead Heritage still uses a mule-powered mill to crush the sorghum cane and cooks the syrup with a wood fire.

Tindell said to keep in mind that grazing is, and must remain, the centerpiece for any type of organic cropping to be viable long term.

"Three years is the absolute maximum time land should remain in crops before returning to leguminous pasture," he said. "Even on our tilled ground we graze the corn stalks after harvest. We graze the wheat in the winter to promote tillering and to prevent freeze damage and we often graze the Southern peas in the summer rather than hand-harvest all of them."

Animals help out in other areas as well. Indian Runner Ducks are used for insect control in the vegetable gardens and chickens and turkeys do the same thing in the vineyard. Geese are excellent weeders in corn and cotton. Even the work stock has become a salable product as there is a healthy demand for the farm's home-raised mules in Texas.

I am hoping that this "Heritage Food" movement that is starting in the Deep South will grow and spread across our country. People everywhere once fed themselves without petroleum inputs by working with what God gave them in their locality. We can do that again.

Health Benefits Of Heritage Foods

The national food writer, Michael Pollan, author of *The Omnivore's Dilemma* and *In Defense of Food*, said that cancer, heart disease and diabetes were virtually unknown 150 years ago. The following may give you some clues why this was so.

Sweet Potatoes—Excellent source of vitamins A, C, and manganese. High in anti-oxidants that help prevent heart disease, diabetic heart disease, and colon cancer. Anti-inflammatory helps prevent asthma, osteoarthritis, and rheumatoid arthritis.

Cane Molasses—Excellent source of iron for menstruating, pregnant or lactating women. Provides more iron from fewer calories than beef. Totally fat-free. Good source of calcium. Helps remove toxins from the colon and may help prevent migraine headaches. Prevents tiredness, muscle cramps, tension and muscle soreness.

Turnip Greens—Excellent source of vitamins A, C, E, B6, folate, copper, calcium, and dietary fiber. Helps prevent rheumatoid arthritis. Vitamin C decreases colon tumors and reduces both colon and rectal cancers. High in anti-oxidants for good heart health.

Whole Grains—Reduces stroke risk by 30-35% and type 2 diabetes by 25-28%. Provides better weight control. Reduces asthma risk. Promotes healthier carotoid arteries, reduces inflammatory diseases, lowers risk of colon-rectal disease, provides for healthier blood pressure, less gum disease and tooth loss.

Onions—Lowers blood sugar, helps prevent diabetes. Good source of chromium, a molecule that helps cells respond appropriately to insulin. Decreases cholesterol and triglyceride levels while increasing "good" HDL cholesterol levels. Research has found 20% decrease in heart disease among onion users.

Garlic—Serves as a natural mosquito repellant. It is a natural antibiotic. Cooked with meat can ward off listeria, salmonella, and E. coli. Eaten fresh can help prevent Crypto-coccal meningitis, Candida albion, Staphylococcus. It is the only anti-bacteria to which bacteria do not build a resistance. Helps prevent blood clots and can reduce blood pressure one to five percent. Reduces chance of a stroke by 30-40% and heart disease by 20-25%.

Radishes—Historical treatment for liver disorders. Contains a variety of sulfur-based chemicals to increase the flow of bile. Helps maintain a healthy gallbladder and liver and improve digestion.

Strawberries—Number one food shown to reduce cancer deaths. Inhibits proliferation of liver cancer cells, helps prevent age-related macular degeneration. Excellent source of vitamin C and manganese. Lessens pain similar to aspirin.

Blueberries—Helps prevent age-related memory loss and malfunction. One cup a day has shown an increase of five to six percent in motor skills in elderly people. Rich source of heart-protective phenols.

Muscadine Wine—Red wine made from Southern native grapes known as muscadine or scuppernong has a much higher level of healthful resveratrol than wines made from other grapes. Resveratrol is a polyphenol anti-oxidant positively linked to inhibiting cancer, heart disease, degenerative nerve disease, viral infections, and mechanism's of Alzheimer's Disease. Muscadine wines may contain more than 40 mg/L of resveratrol. This compares to only 0.2-5.8 mg/L in red wines made from other grapes.

100% Grassfed Meats—A six ounce beef loin from a grassfed animal has about 92 fewer calories than a similar sized loin from a grainfed one. Eating grassfed beef would save the typical American 16,642 calories a year. All things being equal, this one shift will cause you to lose 9.5 pounds over two years. This compares to a loss of 6.4 pounds in two years on Weight Watcher's program. It also has less cholesterol than chicken. Grassfed meats also contain from two to ten times more omega-3 fatty acid than grainfed beef. This is because cool-season grasses are a particularly good source of omega-3 fatty acids. Ruminant animals can produce a newly discovered "good fat" called Conjugated Linoleic Acid (CLA). This fat helps fight two deadly diseases—cancer and cardiovascular disease. There are also encouraging studies showing CLA helps reduce the amount of fatty deposits in arteries by 30 percent, actually reversing the condition. There is from three to six times more vitamin E in grassfed beef than feedlot or grainfed beef and four to six times more beta-carotene.

Full Fat Grassfed Milk—A 1996 study of 4,697 women found that the more full fat milk from pastured cows in a woman's diet the lower her risk of breast cancer. In this study, the women who drank the most milk had a 60 percent lower risk than those who drank the least. In an Irish study, CLA extracted from milk from grassfed cows killed 93 percent of breast cancer cells in just eight days.

Milk and dairy products from pastured cows are higher in beta-carotene, vitamin A and vitamin E as well. The yellow color in industrial cheese and butter comes from Yellow Dye no. 22. In pastured dairy products it comes from beta-carotene.

100% Grassfed Lamb—Today there are only seven million sheep in the United States. In 1925, there were five million between Hattiesburg and the Gulf Coast! Grassfed lamb has more omega-3 fatty acids and CLA than grassfed beef and is particularly rich in lutein, a member of the carotenoid family that helps protect eye health.

Free Foraging Hen Eggs—Eggs from hens raised on pasture for most of the day have ten times more healthful omega-3 in them than eggs from confined hens. Chickens are not vegetarians and enjoy eating insects. These insects help produce the bright orange yolk of free-foraging eggs.

Pastured Poultry—Pastured ducks, geese, and turkeys all have cancer and heart disease fighting CLA in their fat.

Pastured Pigs—Pork from pastured pigs is higher in vitamin E and has more omega-3 fatty acids. The fat from acorn-finished pigs is very similar to that of olive oil and is translucent. The meat from outdoor pigs also has much more vitamin D in the meat than indoor confinement raised pigs.

Bacon Grease—This was the primary cooking oil in Southeast Mississippi until after World War II. It contains less saturated fat, cholesterol, and sodium than the same amount of salted butter. It has the same amount of calories as olive oil, canola oil, and sunflower oil. It was called bacon liquor.

Lard—Dr. Denham Harman studied the effect of various fats and oils on mice. He found that rats fed lard live 9.2% longer than rats fed a polyunsaturate. In humans that translates to almost seven years of life.

Anti-oxidants—Help remove free radicals, which are unstable compounds that damage cell structure increasing the risk of cancer and weakening the immune system. They also protect against eye disease, diabetes and pancreatic disorders, and Alzheimer's disease.

The major anti-oxidant fruits are: Muscadines, blueberries, plums, pomegranates, blackberries, cranberries, and raspberries.

Vitamin A—Prevents night blindness, dandruff, kidney stones, insomnia, depression, acne and itching eyes. Helps ward off infections, especially colds. Aids in building healthy teeth and bones. Prevents the formation of rough hard skin, lung cancer, bladder, and reproductive gland cancer including the prostate.

Good sources are: Fish liver oils, beef liver, cream, free

range eggs, and butter from pastured cows. The yellower the butter the better. Yellow or orange fruits and vegetables, and green, leafy vegetables.

Vitamin B6—Responsible for the proper function of 60 enzymes within our bodies. Plays a major part in the production of hemoglobin and cells within our immune systems. Involved in the breaking down of carbohydrates and their processing to be turned into human energy. Deficiency signs are arthritis, carpal tunnel syndrome, depression and cracked lips.

Food sources are: Bell peppers, turnip greens, spinach, grassfed beef, and cane molasses.

Vitamin C—Aids in wound healing and prevents periodontal disease. It is the most versatile and effective water-soluble dietary anti-oxidant. It is estimated by the U.S. Center for Disease Control that people with adequate vitamin C in their blood live six years longer than those with low levels. Vitamin C lowers blood pressure and LDL "bad Cholesterol." Helps prevent hardening of the arteries.

Food sources are: Cantaloupes, strawberries, green sweet peppers, and red sweet peppers.

Vitamin D—Helps prevent congestive heart failure. Impacts calcium absorption. Helps prevent hip fracture in elderly women. Helps fight infections, particularly the flu. Produces 200 anti-microbial peptides, the most important of which is cathelicidan, a naturally occurring broad-spectrum antibiotic. Thought to help prevent up to 16 cancers. European research found that it lowered the risk of dying from any disease.

Good sources are: Shrimp, unpasteurized grassfed cow's milk, and eggs from free ranging chickens.

Vitamin E—Promotes healing, immune function, and protection from various diseases. Believed to reduce cholesterol and plaque buildup in arteries, thereby reducing the risk of heart disease.

Food sources are: Pecans, peanuts, walnuts, grassfed beef, pastured poultry, and stone ground wheat products.

Index

Index

Index

Bibliography

Aidells, Bruce and Kelly, Denis. *Bruce Adells's Complete Sausage Book: Recipes from America's Premium Sausage Maker*. Ten Speed Press, 2001.

Alexander, Mary Ellen. *Rosalie and Radishes, A history of Long Beach Mississippi*. Gulfport: The Dixie Press, 1980.

Along the Gulf, An entertaining story of an outing among the beautiful resorts on the Mississippi Sound. Originally pub lished by the L&N Railroad in 1895. Republished by Pass Christian Historical Society, 1991.

Bryant, Ralph Clement. *Logging, The Principles and General Methods of Operation in the United States*. Chattanooga, Tennessee: National Model Railroad Association, Inc., 2008.

Dohner, Janet Vorwalk. *The Encyclopedia of Historic and Endangered Livestock and Poultry Breeds*. New Haven and London: Yale University Press, 2001.

Douglass, William Campbell II and MD. *The Milk Book: The Milk of Human Kindness is Not Pasteurized*. Rhino Publishing, S.A., 2004.

Edge, John T. *A Gracious Plenty, Recpies and Recollections from the American South*. New York: HP Books, 1999.

English, Andrew R. *"All Off For Gordon's Station," A History of the Early Hattiesburg, Mississippi Area*. Baltimore, Maryland: Gateway Press, Inc., 2000.

Fallon, Sally. *Nourishing Traditions, The Cookbook that Challenges Politically Correct Nutrition and the Diet Dictocrats*. Washington, D.C.: New Trends Publishing, Inc., 2005.

Fickle, James E. *Mississippi Forests and Forestry*. Jackson: University Press of Mississippi, 2001.

Gore, Laura Locoul. *Memories of the Old Plantation Home*. Vacherie, Louisiana: The Zoë Company, Inc., 2000.

Greenwell, Dale. *Twelve Flags: Triumphs and Tragedies*. Dale Greenwell publisher, 1968.

Hamel, Paul B. & Chitoskey, Mary U. *Cherokee Plants, their*

Bibliography

uses - a 400 year history. Asheville: Hickory Printing, 1982.

"Health Benefits of Vitamin D." *New York Times.com*

"Health Benefits of Vitamins." Wikipedia.

Hickman, Nollie. *Mississippi Harvest, Lumbering in the Longleaf Pine Belt 1840-1915.* University, Mississippi: The University of Mississippi, 1962.

Kurlansky, Mark. *Salt, A World History.* New York: Penguin Books, 2002.

Leslie, Eliza. *Miss Leslie's New Cookery Book.* Philadelphia: T. B. Peterson and Brothers, 1857.

LSU Rural Life Museum, The. *Rural Life Cooks, Traditional Recipes of Louisiana.* Baton Rouge: The LSU Rural Life Museum, 2002.

Mann, Charles C. *1491, New Revelations of the Americas Before Columbus.* New York: Alfred A. Knopf, 2005.

"Mississippi Indians." Jackson: Mississippi Department of Archives and History. Brochure.

McCarty, Kenneth G. Jr., Edited. *Hattiesburg, A Pictorial History.* Jackson: University Press of Mississippi, 1982.

Napier, John Hawkins III. *Lower Pearl River's Piney Woods, Its Land and People.* University, Mississippi: The University of Mississippi, 1985.

Polk, Noel. Ed. *A Human Perspective, Mississippi's Piney Woods.* Jackson: University Press of Mississippi, 1986.

Porcher, Richard Dwight & Fick, Sarah. *The Story of Sea Island Cotton.* Charleston: Wyrick & Company, 2005.

Pyne, Stephen J. *Fire in America, A Cultural History of Wildland and Rural Fire.* Princeton, New Jersey: Princeton University Press, 1982.

Scharff, Robert G. *Louisiana's Loss, Mississippi's Gain, A History of Hancock County, Mississippi From the Stone Age to the Space Age.* Lawrenceville, Virginia: Brunswick Publishing Corporation, 1999.

Service League of Natchitoches, The. *Steel Magnolias in the Kitchen, A Journey through Cane River's Heritage and the Mystery of Southern Charm.* Natchitoches, Louisiana: The

Bibliography

Service League of Natchitoches, 2008.

"Soul Food." Wikipedia.

Stockman Grass Farmer Magazine

Sullivan, Charles L. *The Mississippi Gulf Coast: Portrait of a People, An Illustrated History.* Windsor Publications, Inc., 1985.

Taylor, Roger. *The American Railroad Network 1861-1890.* University of Illinois Press, 2003.

Valentine, Tom. *"Facts on Fats and Oils,"* as noted in *Nourishing Traditions.*

Wells, Mary Ann. *Native Land 1540-1798.* Jackson: The University Press of Mississippi, 1994.

www.braintan.com

www.eatwild.com

www.taxidermy.com

www.universalleather.com

About The Author

Allan Nation has been the editor of *The Stockman Grass Farmer* magazine since 1977. Based in Ridgeland, Mississippi, *The Stockman Grass Farmer* (www.stockmangrassfarmer.com) is an international publication that covers management-intensive grassland enterprises for producers of pasture-raised livestock. This includes stocker cattle, grass finished beef and lamb, and pasture-based dairying. It is the only monthly publication in North America devoted solely to management-intensive grassland farming in all its aspects.

The son of a commercial cattle rancher, Nation grew up in Greenville, Mississippi. He has traveled to some 30 countries studying grassland farming systems. In 1987, he authored a section on Management-intensive Grazing in the *USDA Yearbook of Agriculture* and has served as a consultant and resource for Audubon Society Television Specials, National Geographic, WTBS, PBS, and National Public Radio. He received the 1993 Agricultural Conservation Award from the American Farmland Trust for spearheading the drive behind the grass farming revolution in the United States.

Nation has been a featured speaker at the American Forage and Grasslands Conference, the International Ranching for Profit Conference, the Irish Grasslands Conference, the British Large Herds Conference, the New Zealand Large Herds Conference, the British Grasslands Conference, the Mexican Cattlemen's Association, and the Argentine Agronomy Society. He also delivered the closing remarks at the International Grasslands Conference is Saskatoon, Canada.

He has authored 9 books including *Pa$ture Profit$ with Stocker Cattle, Quality Pasture, Farm Fresh, Knowledge Rich Ranching, Grassfed to Finish,* and *Land, Livestock and Life.*

He lives in Southeast Mississippi with his wife, Carolyn, who is also an author.

To order additional copies of *The Moving Feast*: call 1-800-748-9808 or visit www.stockmangrassfarmer.com